# WHALE

The Dionysus Cup, ancient
Greek, c. 540 B.C.

Krill

Roman coin with
boy riding dolphin,
2nd century B.C.

Ancient Greek
bone figure of dolphin
with coral eye

17th-century engraving of whales
and whaling

Leaping killer
whale, or orca

Common dolphin

Dolphin-shaped
faience vase from
Rhodes, 550
to 500 B.C.

Female California
sea lion

 EYEWITNESS BOOKS

Male walrus

# WHALE

Written by
VASSILI PAPASTAVROU

Photographed by
FRANK GREENAWAY

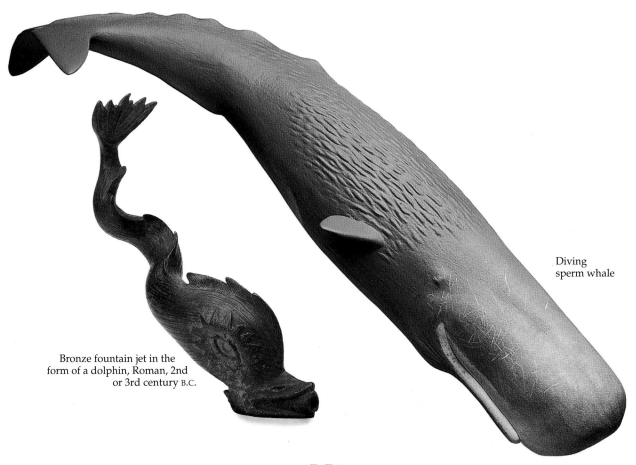

Diving
sperm whale

Bronze fountain jet in the
form of a dolphin, Roman, 2nd
or 3rd century B.C.

Dorling Kindersley

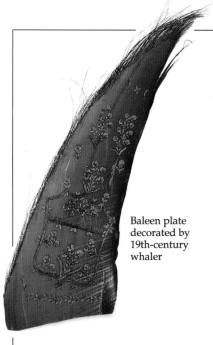

Baleen plate decorated by 19th-century whaler

Upper jaw of extinct whale *Basilosaurus*

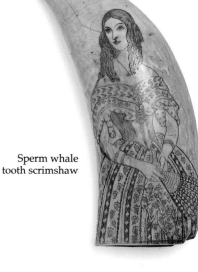

Sperm whale tooth scrimshaw

**DK**

LONDON, NEW YORK,
MELBOURNE, MUNICH, and DELHI

**Project editor** Scott Steedman
**Art editor** Bob Gordon
**Managing editor** Helen Parker
**Managing art editor** Julia Harris
**Researcher** Céline Carez
**Picture research** Sarah Moule
**Production** Catherine Semark
**Live animals photographed at** Marineland, Antibes, France
and Harderwijk Marine Mammal Park, Holland.
**Editorial consultants** Dr Peter Evans and Dr Paul Thompson

First American Edition, 1993
Revised American Edition, 2003

Published in the United States by
DK Publishing, Inc.
375 Hudson Street
New York, New York 10014

03 04 05 10 9 8 7 6

**Library of Congress Cataloging-in-Publication Data**
Papastavrou, Vassili.
Whale / written by Vassili Papastavrou.
p.cm — (Eyewitness Books)
Includes index.
Summary: Describes whales, dolphins, seals, and other marine mammals,
their habitats, means of communication, and family life.
1. Marine mammals—Juvenille literature.
[1. Marine mammals  2. Whales] I. Title.
QL713.2.P37  2000  599.5—dc20  93-856
ISBN 0-7894-5871-3 (pb)    ISBN 0-7894-5870-5 (hc)

Color reproduction by Colourscan, Singapore
Printed in China by Toppan Printing Co. (Shenzhen) Ltd.

Discover more at
**www.dk.com**

Whale meal

Dyed baleen bristles

Spermaceti oil

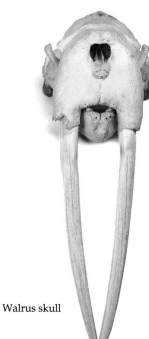

Walrus skull

Narwhal skull with long tusk

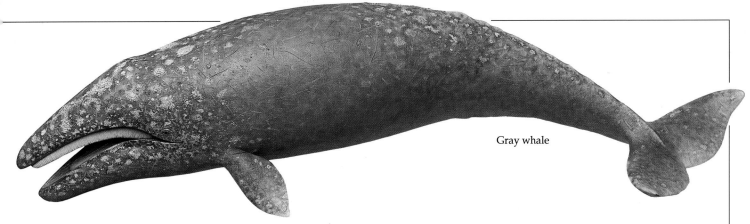

Gray whale

# Contents

# Marine mammals

AT FIRST SIGHT A DOLPHIN looks more like a fish than a person. But like you, the dolphin is a mammal, a warm-blooded animal that feeds its young on mother's milk. It is one of the many kinds of whale, the most successful group of marine mammals. Several other unrelated groups of mammals, including seals and dugongs, also make their homes in salt water. Millions of years ago their ancestors left the land to live in the sea. Over time they evolved to suit their new environment, becoming sleek and streamlined. Unlike fish, which take oxygen from the water, marine mammals must come to the surface regularly to breathe. But taking oxygen from the air is efficient, and most marine mammals are fast swimmers and powerful hunters.

**ARISTOTLE**
Whales are mammals, not fish. The Greek scientist and philosopher Aristotle recognized this 2,400 years ago. He also noticed that they suckle their young and breathe air, like other mammals.

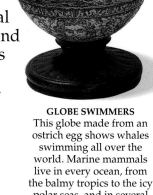

**GLOBE SWIMMERS**
This globe made from an ostrich egg shows whales swimming all over the world. Marine mammals live in every ocean, from the balmy tropics to the icy polar seas, and in several great rivers. Some migrate vast distances to feed and give birth.

**WHALE-SIZED**
In every language, the word for 'whale' connotes something large. Even the smallest whales are the size of a person. This pilot whale weighs 2,850 lb (1,300 kg), about 18 times the size of an adult man. The largest whales are bigger than any dinosaur, and the blue whale, the largest of all, weighs 220 tons (200 tonnes) and is as long as a Boeing 737 jet!

*Layer of fur protects and keeps animal warm*

**FIN FOOT**
Seals, sea lions, and walruses are pinnipeds, which means "fin-footed." They are powerful swimmers superbly adapted to life in the sea. As their name suggests, they have webbed feet. But unlike whales, they have not lost their back legs and have to come ashore to give birth.

*Powerful front flippers used to propel sea lion through water*

**SEA MONSTER**
Whales are mysterious creatures. The biggest species live far out at sea and spend most of their lives under water. Early drawings were based on sailors' stories of sea monsters with huge mouths that huffed and puffed like dragons.

*Webbed back flippers*

_Dorsal fin_

_Blowhole_

## WHALES AND DOLPHINS
Of all marine mammals, the best adapted to life in the sea are the cetaceans, or whales. The group gets its name from the Greek word _ketos_, meaning "sea monster". It includes dolphins and porpoises, which are really whales. This bottle-nosed dolphin is a typical whale. It is a powerful swimmer with strong tail flukes, two pectoral (chest) fins, a dorsal (back) fin, and no hind legs. It breathes through a blowhole on the top of its head.

_Pectoral fins, used to steer while swimming_

_Tough, rubbery skin with very few hairs_

_Swimming muscles that drive the whale through water_

_Flukes, the correct name for a whale's "tail"_

## THAR SHE BLOWS!
No group of animals has been hunted as ruthlessly as whales (pp. 46–51). They were once common in all the world's oceans, but by the middle of this century many populations had been virtually wiped out. The industry declined, and a public outcry helped to control the killing. But many whale populations may never recover (p. 63).

## SEA SIRENS
Like whales, manatees and dugongs have no hind legs and spend their entire lives in the water (pp. 44–45). They are gentle vegetarians, and sailors used to mistake them for mermaids. They are known as sirenians, from the Greek word for mermaid, _seiren_.

_Light color blends in with snow and ice of Arctic_

## SEA BEAR
Are polar bears marine mammals? Probably, because they depend on the sea. For much of the year, polar bears live on the floating ice pack. Hunting on the ice, they ambush seals at air holes. They are superb swimmers but cannot stay under water very long.

_Heavy coat of fur keeps bear warm_

_Powerful paws used to kill prey such as seals_

## SEA OTTER
Most otters are found in rivers, but there are two species that live all the time in salt water. Sea otters entered the oceans relatively recently and are not as well adapted as other marine mammals. They are sleek and streamlined, with dense fur and webbed feet.

# Whale evolution

THE FIRST MAMMALS all lived on land. How or why the ancestors of whales returned to the sea is still unclear. About 55 million years ago, a group of mammals seem to have colonized salty estuaries teeming with fish. Over the millennia, they gradually changed to suit their watery home. Skulls of early whales show how their nostrils moved to the top of the head to make breathing under water easier. Strong tail flukes for swimming evolved, front limbs turned into blades for steering, and back limbs slowly wasted away. Baleen whales have developed a different way of feeding (pp. 24–25), but they probably share the same ancestors as toothed whales. One clue is that they are born with tiny tooth buds that never develop.

**AN EARLY WHALE?**
Most scientists agree that whales have the same ancestors as even-toed ungulates (hoofed animals), which include modern cows and deer. These ancestors lived on land and hunted other animals. This is a model of *Mesonyx*, an odd carnivore that looked like a wolf but had hooves like a cow. Just like today's carnivores, *Mesonyx* had several different kinds of teeth (pp. 22–23).

**OLD WHALE**
The *archæocetes* (from the Latin for "old whales") lived in shallow seas and salty estuaries 55 million years ago. Their nostrils were still at the front of their heads.

Nostrils near front of snout

Variety of teeth, like a modern land mammal

Orbit, cavity for eye

Nostril has moved back along snout

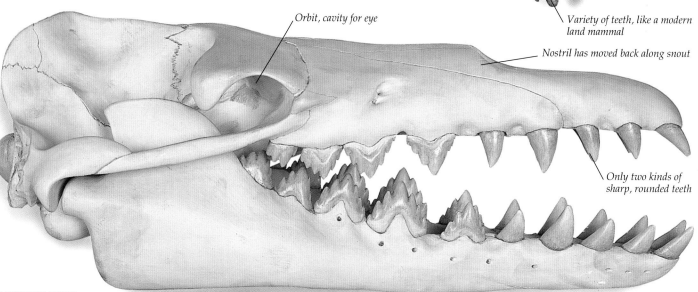

Only two kinds of sharp, rounded teeth

**SEAFOOD PLATTER**
We know almost nothing about how early whales lived. But the teeth give some clues. *Prozeuglodon isis* probably lived in shallow water, where it caught fish and ground up shells to eat the soft-bodied animals within.

**MORE LIKE A DOLPHIN**
In some ways the skull of *Prosqualodon davidi*, which lived 25 million years ago, looks like a modern dolphin's skull (p. 23). Its blowhole must have been near the top of its head, and its teeth are all a similar size and shape.

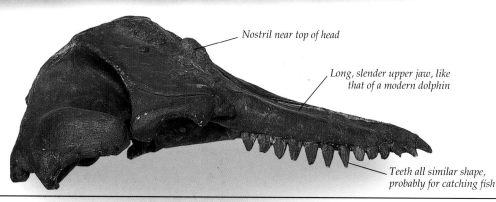

Nostril near top of head

Long, slender upper jaw, like that of a modern dolphin

Teeth all similar shape, probably for catching fish

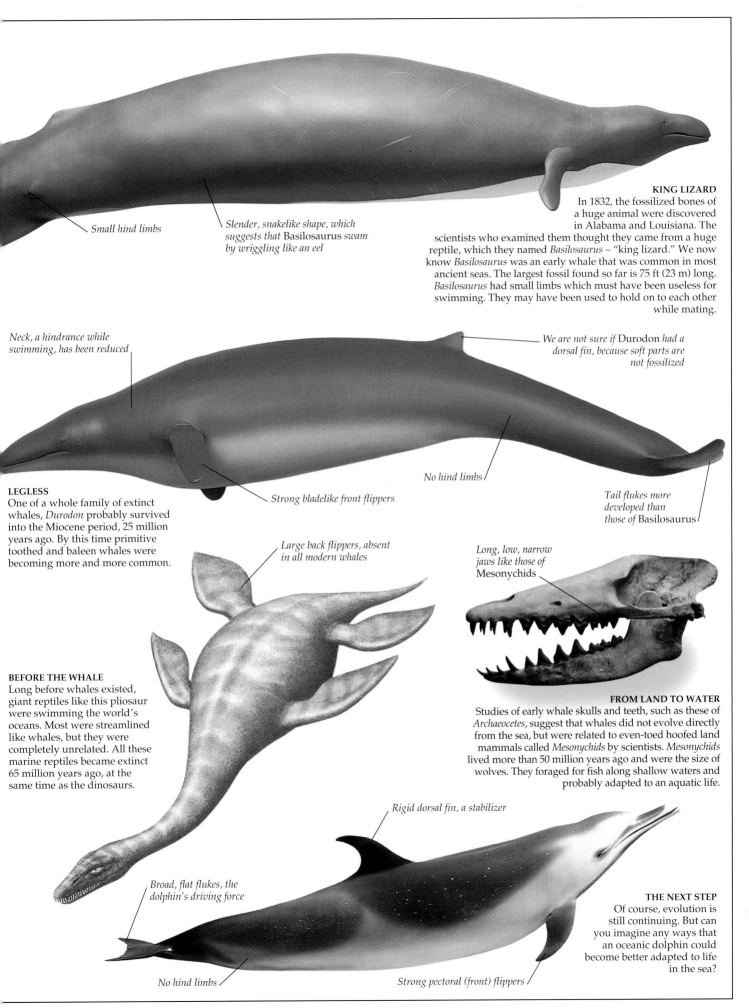

Small hind limbs

Slender, snakelike shape, which suggests that Basilosaurus *swam by wriggling like an eel*

**KING LIZARD**
In 1832, the fossilized bones of a huge animal were discovered in Alabama and Louisiana. The scientists who examined them thought they came from a huge reptile, which they named *Basilosaurus* – "king lizard." We now know *Basilosaurus* was an early whale that was common in most ancient seas. The largest fossil found so far is 75 ft (23 m) long. *Basilosaurus* had small limbs which must have been useless for swimming. They may have been used to hold on to each other while mating.

Neck, a hindrance while swimming, has been reduced

We are not sure if Durodon *had a dorsal fin, because soft parts are not fossilized*

**LEGLESS**
One of a whole family of extinct whales, *Durodon* probably survived into the Miocene period, 25 million years ago. By this time primitive toothed and baleen whales were becoming more and more common.

Strong bladelike front flippers

No hind limbs

Tail flukes more developed than those of Basilosaurus

Large back flippers, absent in all modern whales

Long, low, narrow jaws like those of Mesonychids

**BEFORE THE WHALE**
Long before whales existed, giant reptiles like this pliosaur were swimming the world's oceans. Most were streamlined like whales, but they were completely unrelated. All these marine reptiles became extinct 65 million years ago, at the same time as the dinosaurs.

**FROM LAND TO WATER**
Studies of early whale skulls and teeth, such as these of *Archaeocetes*, suggest that whales did not evolve directly from the sea, but were related to even-toed hoofed land mammals called *Mesonychids* by scientists. *Mesonychids* lived more than 50 million years ago and were the size of wolves. They foraged for fish along shallow waters and probably adapted to an aquatic life.

Rigid dorsal fin, a stabilizer

Broad, flat flukes, the dolphin's driving force

**THE NEXT STEP**
Of course, evolution is still continuing. But can you imagine any ways that an oceanic dolphin could become better adapted to life in the sea?

No hind limbs

Strong pectoral (front) flippers

9

# Whales big and small

**BOTTLE-NOSED DOLPHIN**
Star of the TV show *Flipper* (p. 54), this is the whale most people know best.

Whales are found in every ocean, from the tropics to the icy waters of the Poles, and in five of the world's largest rivers. At a maximum length of 100 ft (30 m) and weight of 220 tons (200 tonnes), the blue whale is the largest animal that has ever lived. At the other end of the scale, the smallest dolphins and porpoises are less than 6 ft (2 m) long. There are about 78 species of whale, in two main groups. The toothed whales, such as the dolphins and the sperm whale, hunt fish and squid (pp. 22–23); the huge baleen whales, such as the blue and fin whales, feed by straining fish and small shrimplike animals from the water (pp. 24–25). Another way to tell them apart is that toothed whales have one blowhole and baleen whales have two (p. 17). Although no species of whale has been driven to extinction, many species have been reduced several to low numbers by whaling, fishing nets, and pollution (pp. 58–59).

*Harbor porpoise*
*North Atlantic Ocean*
*To 6 ft (1.8 m)*

*No beak*

**THE PORPOISE FAMILY**
All six species of porpoise are small, with a maximum length of little more than 6 ft (2 m). They have no beak and can be easily identified from close examination by their spade-shaped teeth. Dall's porpoise lives in deep ocean waters, but the other five stick close to the coast.

**OCEANGOING DOLPHINS**
The largest family of whales, dolphins thrive in every ocean except the cold waters of the Arctic and Antarctic. Most of the 26 species have a similar shape, but some do not have an obvious beak, and two have no dorsal fin. Their distant relatives the river dolphins are found in the fresh waters of the Yangtze, Amazon, Indus, and Ganges rivers (p. 33).

*Dorsal fin curves like a sickle*

*Row of bumps instead of dorsal fin*

*Prominent beak*

*Most dolphin species can be identified by the distinctive patterns on their flanks*

*Scratches from collisions with boats and encounters with sharks and killer whales and of course from each other*

*Common dolphin*
*Oceans and seas worldwide*
*To 8 ft (2.4 m)*

*Powerful tail flukes*

**THE NARWHAL FAMILY**
Sometimes called "the unicorn of the seas", the male narwhal has one of the most remarkable teeth of any animal (pp. 36–37). Like its close relative the beluga, it lives in the icy waters of the Arctic. The third member of this family, the Irrawaddy dolphin, is found far away in tropical Asia. Unlike most other whales, all three species have unfused neck vertebrae, which allow them to turn their heads.

*Narwhal*
*Arctic seas*
*To 15 ft 5 in (4.7 m)*

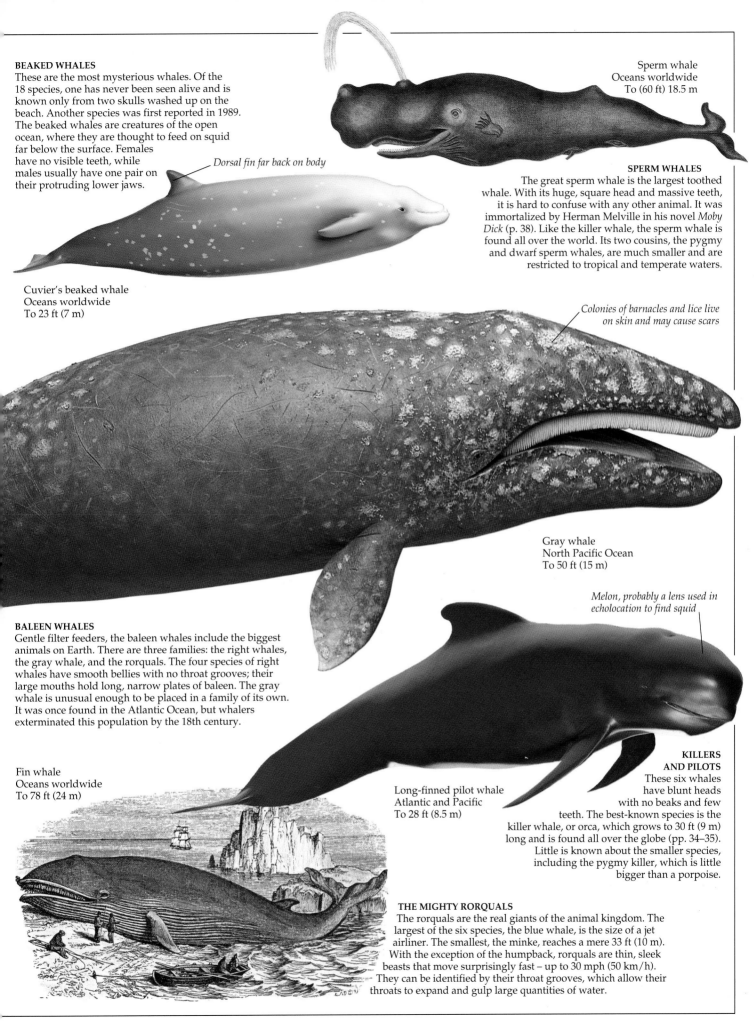

## BEAKED WHALES

These are the most mysterious whales. Of the 18 species, one has never been seen alive and is known only from two skulls washed up on the beach. Another species was first reported in 1989. The beaked whales are creatures of the open ocean, where they are thought to feed on squid far below the surface. Females have no visible teeth, while males usually have one pair on their protruding lower jaws.

*Dorsal fin far back on body*

Cuvier's beaked whale
Oceans worldwide
To 23 ft (7 m)

Sperm whale
Oceans worldwide
To (60 ft) 18.5 m

## SPERM WHALES

The great sperm whale is the largest toothed whale. With its huge, square head and massive teeth, it is hard to confuse with any other animal. It was immortalized by Herman Melville in his novel *Moby Dick* (p. 38). Like the killer whale, the sperm whale is found all over the world. Its two cousins, the pygmy and dwarf sperm whales, are much smaller and are restricted to tropical and temperate waters.

*Colonies of barnacles and lice live on skin and may cause scars*

Gray whale
North Pacific Ocean
To 50 ft (15 m)

## BALEEN WHALES

Gentle filter feeders, the baleen whales include the biggest animals on Earth. There are three families: the right whales, the gray whale, and the rorquals. The four species of right whales have smooth bellies with no throat grooves; their large mouths hold long, narrow plates of baleen. The gray whale is unusual enough to be placed in a family of its own. It was once found in the Atlantic Ocean, but whalers exterminated this population by the 18th century.

*Melon, probably a lens used in echolocation to find squid*

Fin whale
Oceans worldwide
To 78 ft (24 m)

Long-finned pilot whale
Atlantic and Pacific
To 28 ft (8.5 m)

## KILLERS AND PILOTS

These six whales have blunt heads with no beaks and few teeth. The best-known species is the killer whale, or orca, which grows to 30 ft (9 m) long and is found all over the globe (pp. 34–35). Little is known about the smaller species, including the pygmy killer, which is little bigger than a porpoise.

## THE MIGHTY RORQUALS

The rorquals are the real giants of the animal kingdom. The largest of the six species, the blue whale, is the size of a jet airliner. The smallest, the minke, reaches a mere 33 ft (10 m). With the exception of the humpback, rorquals are thin, sleek beasts that move surprisingly fast – up to 30 mph (50 km/h). They can be identified by their throat grooves, which allow their throats to expand and gulp large quantities of water.

# Inside the whale

LIKE A WHALE'S OUTSIDES, its insides are enormous. A blue whale's arteries are as big as drainpipes, and its heart is the size of a small car. Its huge tongue weighs 4.4 tons (4 tonnes). Whales have all the same internal organs as other mammals, but many have been modified to cope with life in the sea. For example, they have huge kidneys, which they need to get rid of excess salt. Whales have no hind limbs. But many species have a few vestigial (left-over) back leg bones, reminders of their ancestors that walked on land (pp. 8–9). Baleen whale skeletons are easily identified by their vast mouths, which allow the whales to gulp enormous quantities of seawater (pp. 24–25).

**BIG MOUTH**
The biggest mouth in the animal kingdom belongs to the blue whale. The huge jaw bones are sometimes erected as arches. This one in the old whaling port of Whitby, England, comes from one of the last blue whales ever caught (pp. 20–21).

**THREE DAYS INSIDE THE WHALE**
The Bible tells the story of Jonah, who found himself on a boat caught in a storm. The frightened crew threw Jonah overboard, and he was swallowed by a whale. After three days, the whale spat him out, still living, onto a beach (p. 55).

*Lumbar (back) vertebrae*

*Tall processes, where powerful swimming muscles join the backbone*

*Chevrons, V-shaped bones attached to bottom of vertebrae*

*Sacral (pelvic) vertebrae*

*Caudal (tail) vertebrae*

Porpoise flipper

*Scapula*

*Humerus*

*Radi*

*Ulna*

*Metacarpals*

*Wr bo*

*Phalanges*

**SMELLY BONES**
In 1830, visitors flocked to the Royal College of London to admire the bones of a huge right whale. Mounting skeletons of this size is a difficult engineering feat. Many of the bones are too heavy for one man to carry, and have to be held in place by strong steel girders. Whale bones contain a lot of oil and are very smelly before they are cleaned.

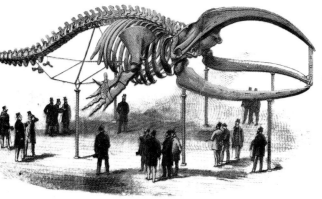

*Scapula (shoulder blade)*

**A WHALE'S ARM**
A person's arm and a porpoise's flipper look very different on the outside. But under the skin are the same bones, adapted over the millennia to their different functions. A human arm is long and thin, designed for climbing or carrying and manipulating objects. The porpoise's flipper, used for steering and braking, is much shorter and stronger.

*Humerus (upper arm bone)*

Human arm

*Radius*

*Ulna*

**SPONGY BONE**
A land mammal's entire weight is held up by its bones, which are hard and strong. But the great weight of a whale is supported by the sea, and its bones have become soft and spongy. This can be seen clearly in Inuit carvings of whale bones, like this sculpture of a seal.

*Wristbones*

*Metacarpals (Hand bones)*

*Phalanges (Finger bones)*

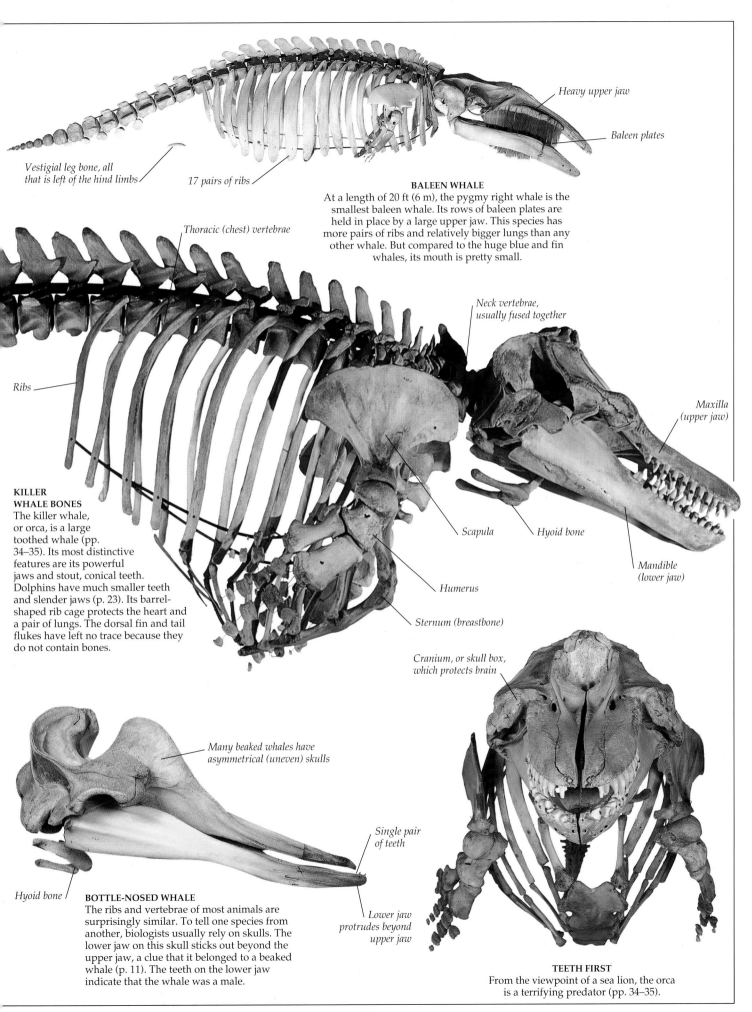

*Heavy upper jaw*

*Baleen plates*

*Vestigial leg bone, all that is left of the hind limbs*

*17 pairs of ribs*

**BALEEN WHALE**
At a length of 20 ft (6 m), the pygmy right whale is the smallest baleen whale. Its rows of baleen plates are held in place by a large upper jaw. This species has more pairs of ribs and relatively bigger lungs than any other whale. But compared to the huge blue and fin whales, its mouth is pretty small.

*Thoracic (chest) vertebrae*

*Neck vertebrae, usually fused together*

*Ribs*

*Maxilla (upper jaw)*

**KILLER WHALE BONES**
The killer whale, or orca, is a large toothed whale (pp. 34–35). Its most distinctive features are its powerful jaws and stout, conical teeth. Dolphins have much smaller teeth and slender jaws (p. 23). Its barrel-shaped rib cage protects the heart and a pair of lungs. The dorsal fin and tail flukes have left no trace because they do not contain bones.

*Scapula*

*Hyoid bone*

*Humerus*

*Mandible (lower jaw)*

*Sternum (breastbone)*

*Cranium, or skull box, which protects brain*

*Many beaked whales have asymmetrical (uneven) skulls*

*Single pair of teeth*

*Hyoid bone*

**BOTTLE-NOSED WHALE**
The ribs and vertebrae of most animals are surprisingly similar. To tell one species from another, biologists usually rely on skulls. The lower jaw on this skull sticks out beyond the upper jaw, a clue that it belonged to a beaked whale (p. 11). The teeth on the lower jaw indicate that the whale was a male.

*Lower jaw protrudes beyond upper jaw*

**TEETH FIRST**
From the viewpoint of a sea lion, the orca is a terrifying predator (pp. 34–35).

# Seals and sea lions

ALL 34 SPECIES OF SEAL are hunters. Most feed on fish, but some, such as the ferocious leopard seal, eat other seals. There are three families: the true, or earless, seals (18 species), the eared seals (15 species), and the walrus, which is unusual enough to go in a family of its own. Seals are found all over the world, but they are most common in the icy waters of the Arctic and Antarctic. This is probably because food supplies are more reliable in the polar regions than in warmer waters. Many species have been reduced to low numbers by human activities. Sealing was just as ruthless as whaling (pp. 52–53), and millions of animals were killed in the last two centuries. Now other seal populations are seriously threatened by pollution (pp. 58-59). Seals spend much of their lives at sea and so are hard to study. Yet new techniques such as satellite tracking (p. 61) are revealing surprising new information about this remarkable and mysterious group of mammals.

### ALL IN THE FAMILY
The largest seal, the male elephant seal, grows to 21 ft (6.5 m) and weighs up to 4.5 tons (4 tonnes). The smallest species, the ringed and Baikal seals, reach 4 ft 6 in (1.37 m) and weigh 140 lb (64 kg).

### HAULED OUT
Seals come onto land or ice to give birth. This is called hauling out. Land-breeding seals like the elephant seal gather at a few popular beaches, where competition between bulls (males) can be intense. Bigger, stronger bulls usually triumph, so bulls are usually much larger than cows (females). Ice-breeding seals like this ringed seal are spread out over a larger area, and bulls and cows are closer to the same size.

### TRUE SEALS
This common, or harbor, seal is a true seal. It has a round, chubby shape and no obvious earflaps. Like all true seals, it cannot turn its hind flippers under its body, so it cannot climb very well on land. But it moves surprisingly fast on rocky shores. This family includes the world's most common marine mammal, the crabeater seal, and the monk seals, which are among the rarest.

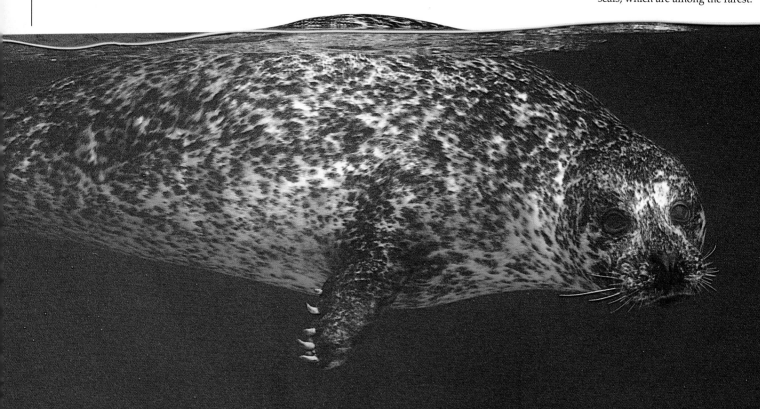

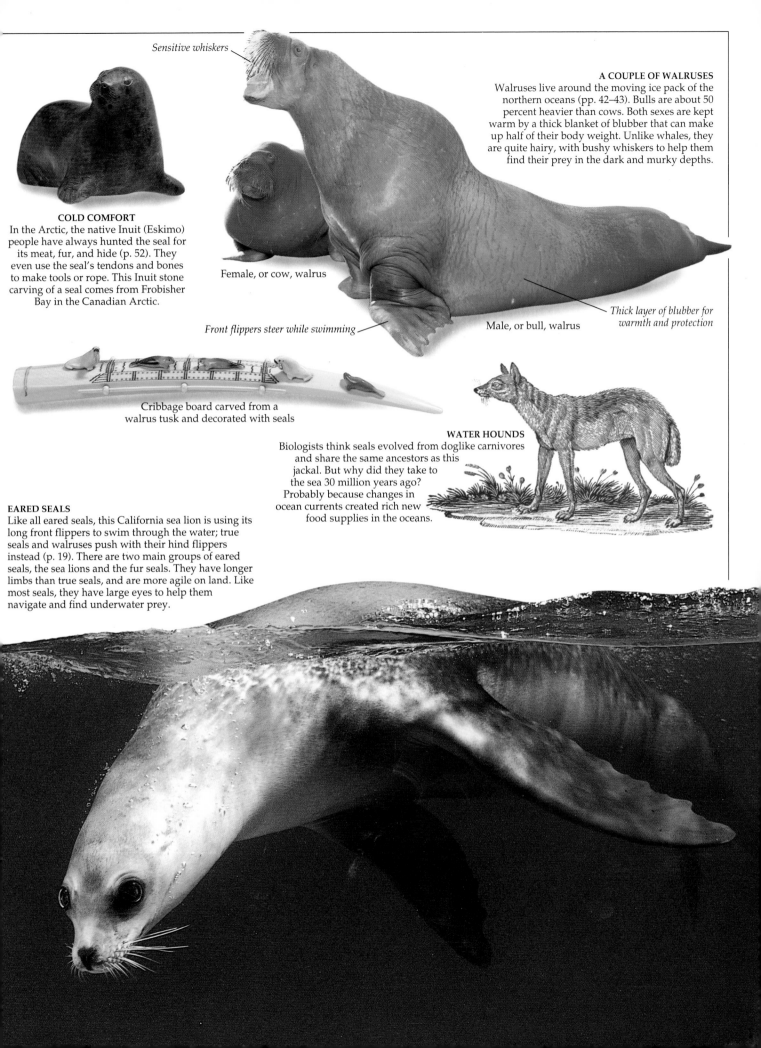

*Sensitive whiskers*

### A COUPLE OF WALRUSES
Walruses live around the moving ice pack of the northern oceans (pp. 42–43). Bulls are about 50 percent heavier than cows. Both sexes are kept warm by a thick blanket of blubber that can make up half of their body weight. Unlike whales, they are quite hairy, with bushy whiskers to help them find their prey in the dark and murky depths.

### COLD COMFORT
In the Arctic, the native Inuit (Eskimo) people have always hunted the seal for its meat, fur, and hide (p. 52). They even use the seal's tendons and bones to make tools or rope. This Inuit stone carving of a seal comes from Frobisher Bay in the Canadian Arctic.

Female, or cow, walrus

*Thick layer of blubber for warmth and protection*

*Front flippers steer while swimming*

Male, or bull, walrus

Cribbage board carved from a walrus tusk and decorated with seals

### WATER HOUNDS
Biologists think seals evolved from doglike carnivores and share the same ancestors as this jackal. But why did they take to the sea 30 million years ago? Probably because changes in ocean currents created rich new food supplies in the oceans.

### EARED SEALS
Like all eared seals, this California sea lion is using its long front flippers to swim through the water; true seals and walruses push with their hind flippers instead (p. 19). There are two main groups of eared seals, the sea lions and the fur seals. They have longer limbs than true seals, and are more agile on land. Like most seals, they have large eyes to help them navigate and find underwater prey.

# Suited to life in the sea

**W**HALES AND SEALS ARE SUPERBLY SUITED to life in the sea. Because they are supported by the water, they do not need strong legs, and they have evolved a sleek shape that slides easily through the water. Many species can swim as fast as a small boat. Powerful muscles in the tail and flanks drive them forward. Their fins are also streamlined, like a plane's wings. Water is a cold home, and almost all whales and seals have thick layers of blubber which keep them very warm. Many seals also have heavy, oily fur which traps bubbles of air and keeps the animals warm and dry.

**DIVING IN**
In most of the world, the ocean is cold enough to take your breath away. In polar seas, a human would barely survive a minute. Water is a very good conductor of heat, so an animal loses heat 25 times faster in water than in the air.

*Long guard hairs*　　*Fine underfur*

**A LINED COAT**
A close look at a fur seal's coat reveals two kinds of hair. The longer, thicker hairs protect the seal as it scrapes against the rocks. But it is air bubbles caught in the fine, dense underfur that keep the seal warm.

**SUNBATHING**
Seals and sea lions often bask in the sun to warm up. But they are so well insulated that they can easily get too hot. When this happens, they cool off by waving their front flippers in the air or burying them in the sand. When northern elephant seals overheat, they flip cool sand over their backs (pp. 40–41).

Female California sea lion

Male California sea lion

**FAT FOOD**
A whale's fat or blubber does not just warm and protect it. It is also a food store. When a right whale is feeding, its blubber may grow to 2 ft (60 cm) thick. The whale can then live off its blubber during the long periods when it does not eat at all.

**NOT HALF FAT**
Walruses have a lot of fat! As much as half of their body weight is blubber. The rolls of fat keep them warm in the freezing seas and ice floes of the Arctic. Thousands of walruses were once killed for their blubber, which was boiled and turned into oil (p. 53).

*When a walrus is too hot, tiny blood vesssels in the skin fill with blood and the animal seems to blush*

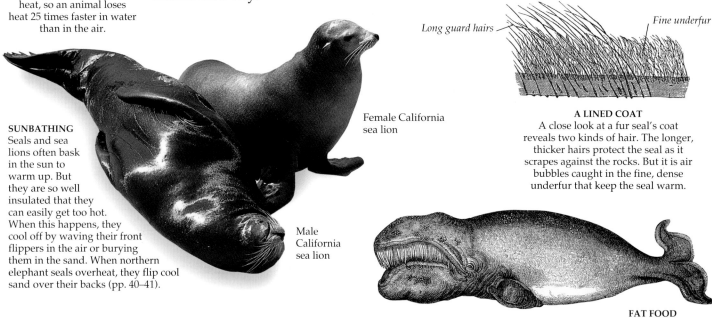

**KEEPING YOUR HEAD ABOVE WATER**
Humans are poor swimmers. They have no flippers or tail flukes, and get cold because they have hardly any fat. They can barely hold their breath for more than a minute, and have to stick their mouths out of the water to gulp air. Whales have solved all these problems. They have even evolved blowholes that allow them to breathe through the top of the head.

**OPEN...**
A whale's blowhole is a modified nostril that sits on top of its head. Toothed whales like this orca have only one blowhole. This opens so the whale can snort the old air out of its huge pair of lungs.

**... AND CLOSED**
Muscles force the blow-hole shut before the orca submerges.

*Massive, broad pectoral fin*

# Coming up to breathe

Taking a breath at sea is a difficult business. Under water, a whale's blow-hole or a seal's nostrils are shut tight. When the whale surfaces, it breathes out very rapidly. The "blow" forms a fine mist of spray up to 13 ft (4 m) high that can be seen miles away. A moment later, the whale breathes in and submerges. Seals breathe out and dive with empty lungs.

**DOUBLE-BARRELED**
Baleen whales have two blowholes that sit side-by-side. Their blow usually looks like a single spray of mist. Only right whales produce distinctive double blows. This minke whale's blow is almost invisible, except in the very coldest Antarctic waters.

*Umbilicus (belly button)*

*Genital slit*

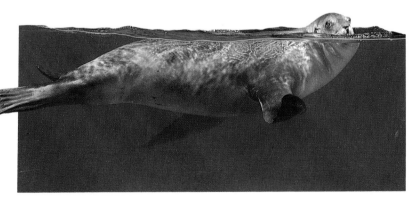

*Anus*

**SEAL SOLUTIONS**
A seal's eyes and nostrils are at the top of its head, so they stick out of the water while it swims along. Seals and sea lions can even sleep at sea. Some species sleep under water and somehow manage to wake up every few minutes to breathe. Other kinds of seals sleep at the surface with their nostrils poking out of the water like a snorkel. This is called bottling.

**TORPEDO-SHAPED**
Land animals come in all shapes and sizes. This is because they move in air, which hardly provides any resistance. But swimming through water is hard work, and marine animals all have a similar, stream-lined shape. Even their sexual organs, which would slow them down, are tucked away in a genital slit.

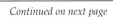

 *Continued on next page*

*Long pectoral fin, or flipper*

*Throat grooves, a clue that
the humpback is a rorqual*

### ON A WING AND A SONG
This leaping humpback is showing off its
graceful flippers, much longer than any
other whale's. These are much too long for
simple steering, and are sometimes used to
rub other whales. Humpbacks also slap their flippers
on the water, to make loud splashing noises. This is
called flippering.

### TICKET TO RIDE
Barnacles make their homes on the skin of slow-
moving whales such as right and gray
whales. Rorquals such as the blue
whale are too fast for most hangers-
on. Sperm whales are slow, but
they regularly shed huge
sheets of dead skin. This
makes it hard for other
animals to hitch a free ride
for long.

## Finding their way around
Whales and seals live in a world that is very different
from our own. Even in the clearest ocean water
visibility is rarely more than 100 ft
(30 m), and they have to hunt at
night or in murky water. Seals
rely on sensitive whiskers.
Toothed whales have
developed a system of echolocation, using sounds to
find food and their way
around (pp. 26–27). How
whales navigate when they
migrate thousands of miles is
another question. They may
have a special magnetic sense
and a built-in compass.

*Earflap*

*Nose like a dog's*

*Large eyes*

*Long whiskers,
specialized hairs used
in close quarters*

### EYEBALL TO EYEBALL
In the murky ocean, eyes are less useful than
they are on land. This gray whale's eyes are
not much larger than a cow's. They must be
pretty useless while the whale is feeding on
the muddy ocean bottom. But gray whales
spy hop – stick their heads out of the water
to have a look around.

### HEAD FULL OF SENSES
For their size, seals have much bigger eyes than whales. Their
senses are similar to a dog's. Apart from the walrus (pp. 42–43),
seals can all see well in and out of the water. This California sea
lion has large eyes and good vision even in dim light.
Its nose is very doglike. The long whiskers are especially
useful in dark or murky waters.

*These muscles contract
to pull tail up*

Upstroke begins

Upstroke

Downstroke begins

### FISHY TAIL
A fish's tail is vertical, not
horizontal like a whale's. It moves
its tail from side to side to swim.

*These muscles
contract to pull tail down*

# Swimming power

Whales are incredible swimmers. Underneath their blubber are huge muscle blocks. The killer whale has been clocked at 34 mph (56 km/h), faster than any other sea mammal. Other species travel thousands of miles in their seasonal migrations. The gray whale makes the longest journey, from Mexico to its feeding grounds off Alaska and back again, a round trip of more than 12,000 miles (20,000 km).

*A whale's tail has many tiny blood vessels and works like a car radiator to cool the animal down*

**DRIVING FORCE**
Like a boat's propeller, a whale's tail drives it through the water. Its flukes – the propeller's blades – are flat and rigid. The whale pulls its flukes up and down with large muscles connected to the top and bottom of the spine (p. 12). The whole back third of a killer whale is solid swimming muscle.

*Skin covered in a film of oil that helps whale slide through water*

*Skin feels smooth and rubbery, like a hard-boiled egg*

**MOSTLY MUSCLE**
Do not be fooled by their blubbery appearance. Seals are powerful swimmers, though they cannot compete with whales. Under the fat, this gray seal is mostly muscle.

Open to brake

Closed for cruising

**FRONT FLIPPER DRIVE**
Like all eared seals (p. 15), fur seals swim with their large front flippers. The rear flippers help to steer. On land, the fur seal can tuck them under its body, so it can waddle around. Like dolphins, some seals "porpoise" – that is, leap out of the water when they are swimming fast.

**REAR FLIPPER DRIVE**
True seals (p. 14) swim by moving their back flippers and tail from side to side. Young seals sometimes swim by moving both back flippers together. But adult seals usually move them one at a time. True seals of all ages steer with their front flippers.

Upstroke begins again

Downstroke ends

**THE GREAT SWIMMER**
Dolphins are fast and graceful swimmers. People have always admired the apparent ease with which they glide through the water. Dolphins swim by moving their strong tails up and down. Both the upstroke and the downstroke generate power. But dolphins can swim really fast only in short bursts. A close look at a dolphin's skin shows rows of microscopic ridges. It is not clear how these corrugations help the dolphin; they may reduce turbulence at high speed.

Downstroke

*Front flippers used only for steering*

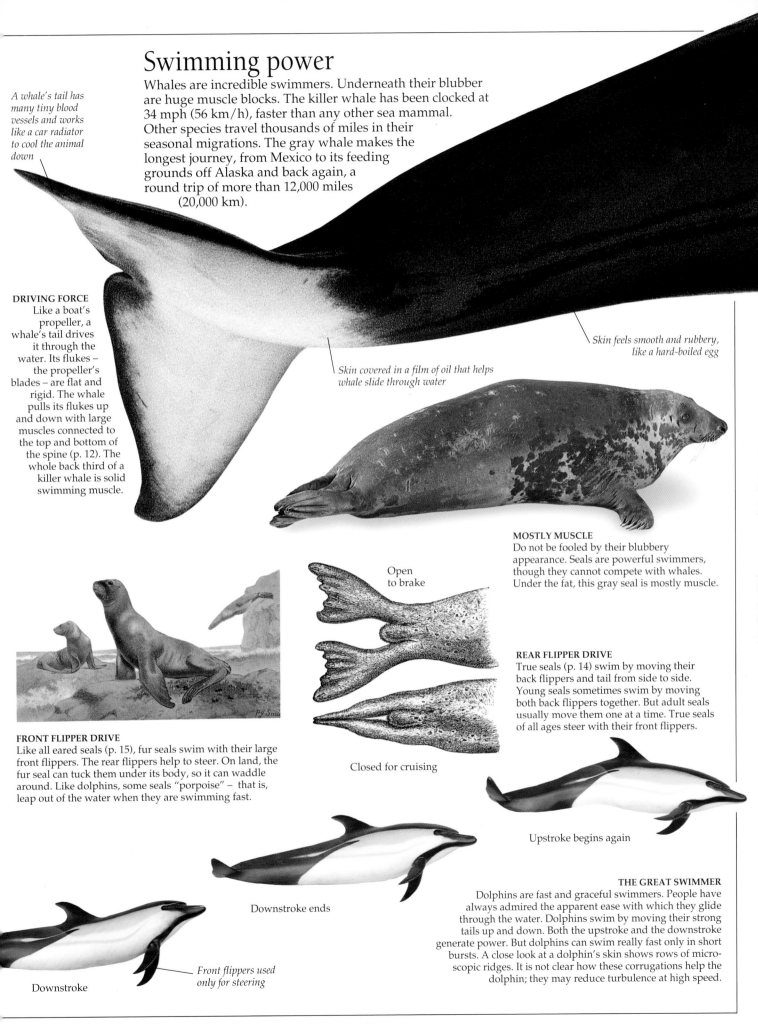

# Ocean giants

THE BIGGEST WHALE – and the biggest animal that has ever lived – is the blue whale. Only other baleen whales and the sperm whale come anywhere near its enormous size. The largest living land animal, the bull elephant, could stand on a blue whale's tongue! Even the biggest dinosaur weighed less than a quarter of a large blue whale. Such size has its benefits. Big animals are less likely to be attacked by predators, and it is easier for them to keep warm. The big problem is finding enough food to nourish their awesome bulk.

*Pectoral fin*

*Tail flukes*

**WHALE LICE**
A number of animals make their homes on the great expanse of a whale's skin. Some are harmless hangers-ons, but others, like this whale louse, probably irritate the skin.

**TALL TAIL**
Unlike some baleen whales, blue whales raise their tails in the air when they dive.

*Stubby dorsal fin*

**A WHALE OF A SHARK**
It is no coincidence that whale sharks, the world's largest fish, are also filter feeders. Because animals that feed on plankton do not need to chase individual prey, they do not have to be agile. This has allowed some to grow to great sizes. Whale sharks do not have baleen plates. Instead, they filter food from the water with their gills.

**THE WORLD'S BIGGEST BABY**
The day it is born, a baby blue whale is already as big as an elephant. It has no baleen plates, and relies entirely on its giant mother's milk. Like seal milk, this is very high in fat. Every day the growing whale drinks about 175 pints (100 litres) of milk and puts on another 200 lb (90 kg). By the time it is weaned, at age six or seven months, the young blue whale is already 54 ft (16 m) long.

## WHALE OUT OF WATER

Whales can reach such incredible sizes only because their weight is supported by the water. When a large whale such as this sperm whale is stranded (pp. 56–57), it cannot support its own weight and its internal organs are crushed.

## BLUE SPLASH

No one knows why whales leap out of the water, or breach. Adults often breach in the company of other whales. This suggests that the big splash is a way of communicating (p. 27). Young animals such as this baby blue may start breaching when they are only a few weeks old. Perhaps by playing they are learning skills which will be important to them as adults.

*Paired blowholes*

## THE BIG BLUE

Blue whales grow to more than 100 ft (32 m) and weigh up to 220 tons (200 tonnes). But we cannot be sure of the exact size of the biggest individuals. Blue whales were hunted mercilessly in the southern oceans, and most of the information on them comes from the whaling industry. Weights were estimated by measuring chopped-off chunks and adding a few tons to make up for lost blood. Even the lengths may be incorrect, as the whales could have been stretched by towing. Blue whales received complete protection from whalers in 1966. But there are no signs that numbers have increased, and there may be only a few hundred left in the entire southern oceans (p. 63).

*Throat grooves, which allow baleen whales to gulp huge amounts of water*

## PILOT STUDY

Measuring a stranded whale is easy. But how do you measure a live whale at sea? One way is to take a series of photos as the whale surfaces. By lining them end to end, scientists can piece together the animal's entire length.

# Teeth for grasping...

MOST WHALES AND SEALS are hunters that catch their slippery prey with rows of sharp teeth. Like most meat-eating mammals (including people), seals and sea lions have a range of different teeth. They grasp their food with powerful canines and incisors and then chew it up with premolars and molars. But toothed whales have simple, peglike teeth that are all the same shape. Teeth are also used for fighting. One of the most amazing teeth of all, the male narwhal's tusk, is probably used to establish dominance over other males (pp. 36–37). Some beaked whales have teeth that are so strangely shaped that it is hard to imagine what they are for (p. 13)! Perhaps the simple sight of the male's huge teeth makes him irresistible to female whales.

**MYSTERY TOOTH**
Only mature male sperm whales have teeth. These are huge, up to 10 in (25 cm) long. How females and young males manage to feed and what males use their teeth for are mysteries.

**ATLANTIC MACKEREL**
Dolphins and seals eat a wide range of fish, from bottom-dwelling cod to fast mackerel like this one. Many dolphins hunt cooperatively.

**LEOPARD OF THE SEAS**
Leopard seals are fierce predators that feed on penguins and even other species of seal. They also strain krill through their teeth, like crabeater seals (p. 25).

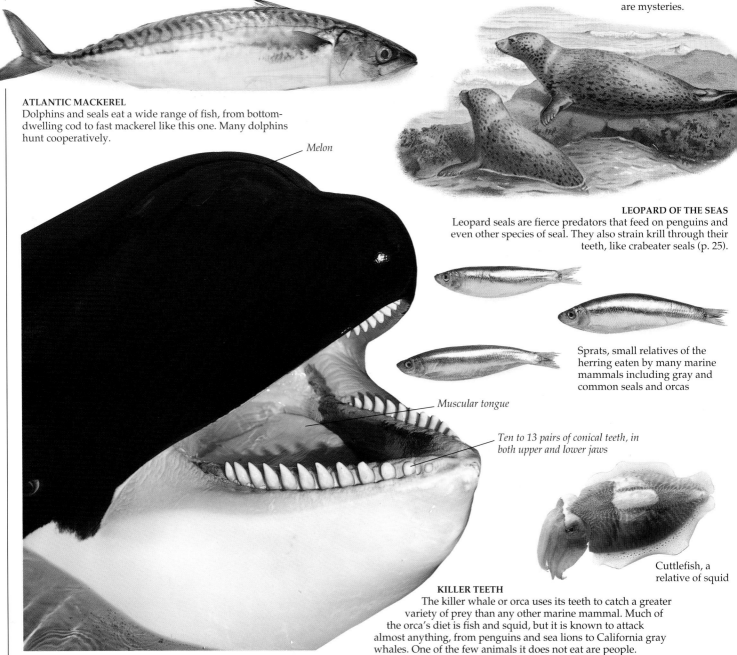

*Melon*

*Muscular tongue*

*Ten to 13 pairs of conical teeth, in both upper and lower jaws*

Sprats, small relatives of the herring eaten by many marine mammals including gray and common seals and orcas

Cuttlefish, a relative of squid

**KILLER TEETH**
The killer whale or orca uses its teeth to catch a greater variety of prey than any other marine mammal. Much of the orca's diet is fish and squid, but it is known to attack almost anything, from penguins and sea lions to California gray whales. One of the few animals it does not eat are people.

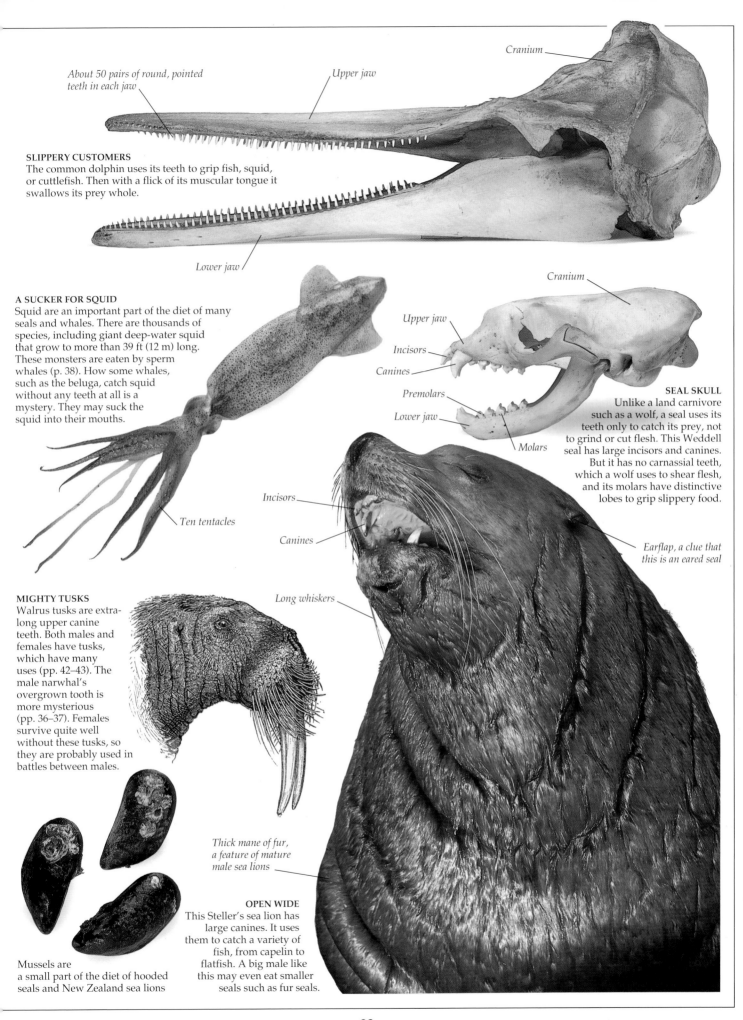

Cranium

About 50 pairs of round, pointed
teeth in each jaw

Upper jaw

**SLIPPERY CUSTOMERS**
The common dolphin uses its teeth to grip fish, squid,
or cuttlefish. Then with a flick of its muscular tongue it
swallows its prey whole.

Lower jaw

**A SUCKER FOR SQUID**
Squid are an important part of the diet of many
seals and whales. There are thousands of
species, including giant deep-water squid
that grow to more than 39 ft (12 m) long.
These monsters are eaten by sperm
whales (p. 38). How some whales,
such as the beluga, catch squid
without any teeth at all is a
mystery. They may suck the
squid into their mouths.

Cranium

Upper jaw

Incisors

Canines

Premolars

Lower jaw

Molars

**SEAL SKULL**
Unlike a land carnivore
such as a wolf, a seal uses its
teeth only to catch its prey, not
to grind or cut flesh. This Weddell
seal has large incisors and canines.
But it has no carnassial teeth,
which a wolf uses to shear flesh,
and its molars have distinctive
lobes to grip slippery food.

Ten tentacles

Incisors

Canines

Earflap, a clue that
this is an eared seal

**MIGHTY TUSKS**
Walrus tusks are extra-
long upper canine
teeth. Both males and
females have tusks,
which have many
uses (pp. 42–43). The
male narwhal's
overgrown tooth is
more mysterious
(pp. 36–37). Females
survive quite well
without these tusks, so
they are probably used in
battles between males.

Long whiskers

Thick mane of fur,
a feature of mature
male sea lions

**OPEN WIDE**
This Steller's sea lion has
large canines. It uses
them to catch a variety of
fish, from capelin to
flatfish. A big male like
this may even eat smaller
seals such as fur seals.

Mussels are
a small part of the diet of hooded
seals and New Zealand sea lions

# ... and baleen for filtering

SOME OF THE BIGGEST WHALES feed by filtering. Their filters are baleen plates, huge fringed brushes that hang inside their mouths like giant sieves. The three families of baleen whales have evolved different filtering techniques. But they all draw seawater into their mouths and spit it back out through the baleen, trapping any tasty morsels on the inside. Some feed mainly on krill, small shrimplike animals found in huge numbers in the southern oceans. Others gulp down entire schools of fish. Most baleen whales pack a whole year's feeding into four or five summer months. In this time their weight may increase by 40 percent. Much of the energy is stored as fat in preparation for the long migrations to winter breeding grounds (p. 19).

**ANOTHER FILTERER**
Like whales, flamingos are filter feeders. They have fringed beaks similar to baleen plates which they skim through the mud upside down.

**BIG GULP**
Rorquals have throat grooves which allow them to expand their mouths to engulf huge quantities of water. A blue whale can take in 66 tons (60 tonnes) of water in one gulp. Then the whale forces the water out by closing its mouth and contracting the grooves. Anything too large to pass through the baleen filter is trapped on the inside and swallowed.

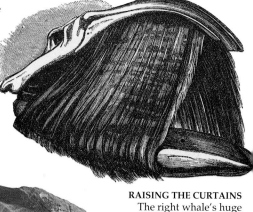

**RAISING THE CURTAINS**
The right whale's huge head contains 200 to 270 pairs of baleen plates. These hang from the whale's upper jaw like two great curtains with the fringes facing inward.

Blowhole

Upper jaw curves to hold long length of baleen

Section cut away to show baleen plates with fringes facing inside mouth

Massive lower lip

Callosities, areas of rough, horny skin infested with barnacles and lice

The right whale's head can make up a quarter of its body length

**SKIMMERS AND GROVELERS**
Right whales usually feed by swimming slowly along with lips parted. Water flows in the front and out the sides of the mouth. Unlike rorquals, they do not open their mouth very wide, but their high, curved lips can hold much longer baleen plates. These are protected by huge lower lips, up to 16 ft (5 m) high in large individuals. The gray whale, the other kind of baleen whale, swims along the bottom making troughs in the mud like a bulldozer. Bowhead whales, a kind of right whale, have been seen feeding in both ways.

*Hard outer edge*

*Inner fringe*

**FIN WHALE BALEEN**
Like your hair and fingernails, baleen is made of a substance called keratin. It grows continually, replacing the fringe as it is worn away.

**FINE FILTER**
A right whale's baleen grows to 14 ft (4.3 m), much longer than that of any other whale. The extremely fine hairs can trap very small animals.

*Top attaches to whale's upper jaw*

**FITTING TOGETHER**
Baleen plates grow from ridges like the ones you can feel on the roof of your mouth. They fit together like cards in a deck.

*Baleen plate decorated by 19th-century whaler*

**KRILL**
Krill are shrimplike creatures no longer than your finger. In the summer they occur in enormous swarms that can cover miles of the southern oceans, where they are the main food for most baleen whales.

*Incisors*

*Canines*

*Cheek teeth with three lobes trap krill in mouth*

**SIEVING SEAL**
Despite its name, the crabeater seal does not eat crabs! Instead it uses its strangely shaped teeth to filter krill from the water. This unusual tactic must be successful, because there are more crabeater seals in the world than any other species of seal.

*Fine fringe where prey is trapped*

*Upper jaw of first whale*

*Upper jaw of second whale*

*Baleen plate*

**BLOWING BUBBLES**
In some parts of the world, humpback whales use bubbles to herd fish together. This is known as bubble netting. The whale swims in a spiral under the fish, blowing bubbles all the time. Then with its mouth wide open it surfaces in the middle and gulps down the whole school. Humpbacks feed alone or in groups of up to 25 animals. These two are fishing together in the cold waters of the Antarctic.

*Lower jaw of first whale, bulging with water and fish*

# Clicks, barks, and songs

SOUND TRAVELS WELL in water, and the seas are noisy places. Whales and seals live in a world dominated by sound. Dolphins coordinate their hunts with whistles and clicks, and male humpbacks sing to attract females. Most large whales make sounds by slapping the surface or breaching – leaping out of the water and coming down with a splash. These splashes can be heard for miles and are probably a kind of communication. The most sophisticated use of sound is in echolocation. Only toothed whales and bats have perfected this skill. By sending out a pulse of sound and listening to the returning echo, whales can find their way around and locate fish and squid in the dark water. The biggest toothed whale, the sperm whale, may even stun squid with loud clicks (pp. 38–39). Baleen whales also make loud sounds. Early sailors were terrified when they heard strange rumbles and groans through the hulls of their wooden ships. We are just beginning to understand these low-frequency calls, which may travel hundreds of miles through the seas.

**EAR BONE**
From the outside, a small pinprick is the only sign of a whale's ear. This dense bone is part of a baleen whale's inner ear.

**SIGNATURE WHISTLE**
Every dolphin makes its own, unique whistle. Scientists listen to these "signature whistles" to identify individuals. Mothers and their calves have similar-sounding whistles.

**WHISTLING WALRUS**
Seals that mate in the water make elaborate underwater sounds. Among the noisiest of all are male walruses courting females. Their songs include loud gongs, like underwater bells. They also rise out of the water to bark, whistle, growl, and clack their teeth.

**HUMPBACK HITS**
Humpback whales are the only nonhumans to make it into the music charts. Many people enjoy listening to the soothing sounds of humpbacks, belugas, and killer whales. A recording of humpback songs was put aboard the *Voyager* space probe as a greeting from Planet Earth.

**LOVE SONG**
The male humpback whale sings a beautiful, haunting song for hours on end. All alone, he sings floating motionless in the water with his head hanging down. Like a lot of male birds, humpbacks sing to attract females. The song consists of a number of phrases repeated over and over again. Each individual sings his own song, slightly different from any other, which evolves slowly from year to year. Whales from different areas sing distinctive themes, so scientists can tell which population a whale comes from by its song.

**BARKING SEA LION**
Seals and sea lions bark a lot. A bark can have many meanings. Male California sea lions bark to frighten off other males. If a female elephant seal (pp. 40–41) is about to be mated by a small male, she will bark to attract the attention of the dominant male, who rushes over and chases away the small male. Seal mothers and pups bark to find each other on the crowded beach (p. 31).

**MOBY CLICK**
When sperm whales get together, they often repeat slow patterns of clicks, called codas. When one whale produces a particular coda, another will repeat it in turn. Sperm whales have huge brains (pp. 38–39). But it is hard to imagine that they can say anything very complicated with such simple clicks.

Two-ton killer whale, or orca

**WAILING IT OUT**
When famous Italian opera singer Luciano Pavarotti sings, he is forcing air past vocal cords that vibrate in his throat. The air leaves through his mouth, so he has to pause every few seconds to breathe in. But whales have no vocal cords, and humpbacks can warble for half an hour between breaths. To do this they must be able to recycle air. Some dolphins can even whistle and echolocate at the same time.

**OUT OF THE WATER...**
Why do whales breach? The loud splashes can be heard many miles away, and are probably a way of communicating. Whales probably slap the water with their tails (lobtailing, p. 38) or flippers (p. 18) for the same reason.

**...AND DOWN WITH A SPLASH!**
Whales are more likely to breach when they are with other whales, and humpbacks breach more in rough weather than calm. This may be the only way to make themselves heard above the water noise.

*Melon, a waxy bulge in the forehead, which may be a lens to focus sounds*

*Blowhole*

*Clicks produced in nasal sacks, bulges in nasal tubes below blowhole*

*Lower jaw may be used to receive echo*

*Echoes "heard" through inner ear, where lower jaw meets skull*

**SOUND SENSATION**
Dolphins produce trains of clicks for echolocation. These can sound like buzzes or doors creaking. But don't be fooled by this open mouth; dolphins produce sounds in nasal sacks beneath their blowholes. Echolocation is an incredibly precise sense. Blindfolded, dolphins can still find objects or distinguish between two balls of slightly different sizes. They may also make loud bangs to stun fish.

# Courtship and birth

THE URGE TO REPRODUCE is strong, and takes up a lot of a whale's or a seal's time and energy. Seals risk the danger of coming ashore to find a mate and give birth. In many species of whale and seal, the males compete for females, with the winning (dominant) males mating with many females. In these species, the males are usually bigger than the females. The most amazing example of this is the elephant seal, where big males are 10 times bigger than females (pp. 40–41). Whales and seals usually mate and give birth in the spring, so their pregnancies last a year. Most seals have a pup every year, but many species of whale raise only one calf every 3 or even 10 years.

**THE RIGHT STUFF**
In winter, southern right whales gather in shallow bays to mate. Several males mate with each female, one after another. The only way a female can escape is by plunging her head under water and sticking her tail in the air. The males just wait, because they know that sooner or later she will have to take a breath.

**ICE BREEDER**
A seal's link with land may be brief. Common seals are born at low tide and swim off before the tide is high again. This hooded seal has a huge choice of ice floes to haul out on, so females are not crowded into a small area. Males are usually seen with only one female at a time. But each female is probably mated by several males, one after another.

**TUSK, TUSK!**
There is usually a lot of bluffing and counterbluffing when males compete. In most species, full-blown fights are rare. These male walruses are fighting for a spot in the water close to a herd of females. A lot is at stake. The winner may mate with more than a dozen females; the loser may never mate at all.

*Female walrus, identified by her smaller size and darker color*

*The walrus's pregnancy lasts 15 to 16 months, longer than any other seal's*

**LOVE IN A COLD CLIMATE**
Walruses have a long and intimate courtship. Males seduce females with barks, growls, and haunting whistles (p. 26). A female who is impressed by his love song will slip off with a male. This female (left) and male (right) are rubbing mustaches. Each female mates with only one male. Mating takes place in the water.

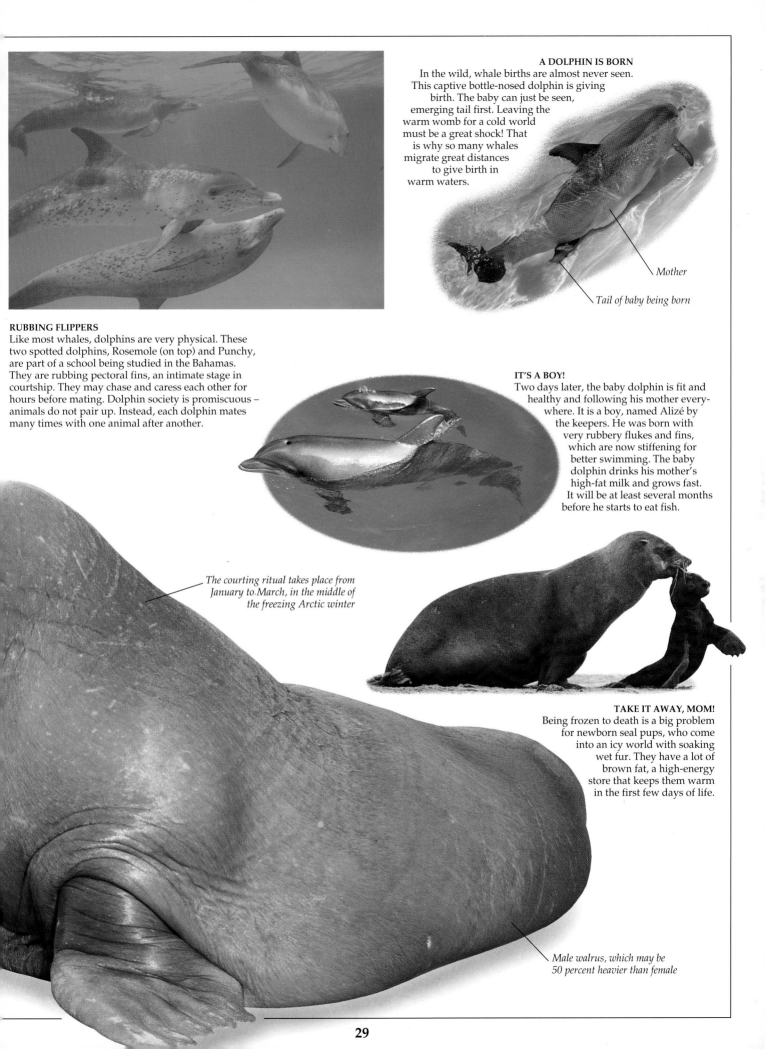

## A DOLPHIN IS BORN
In the wild, whale births are almost never seen. This captive bottle-nosed dolphin is giving birth. The baby can just be seen, emerging tail first. Leaving the warm womb for a cold world must be a great shock! That is why so many whales migrate great distances to give birth in warm waters.

*Mother*

*Tail of baby being born*

## RUBBING FLIPPERS
Like most whales, dolphins are very physical. These two spotted dolphins, Rosemole (on top) and Punchy, are part of a school being studied in the Bahamas. They are rubbing pectoral fins, an intimate stage in courtship. They may chase and caress each other for hours before mating. Dolphin society is promiscuous – animals do not pair up. Instead, each dolphin mates many times with one animal after another.

## IT'S A BOY!
Two days later, the baby dolphin is fit and healthy and following his mother everywhere. It is a boy, named Alizé by the keepers. He was born with very rubbery flukes and fins, which are now stiffening for better swimming. The baby dolphin drinks his mother's high-fat milk and grows fast. It will be at least several months before he starts to eat fish.

*The courting ritual takes place from January to March, in the middle of the freezing Arctic winter*

## TAKE IT AWAY, MOM!
Being frozen to death is a big problem for newborn seal pups, who come into an icy world with soaking wet fur. They have a lot of brown fat, a high-energy store that keeps them warm in the first few days of life.

*Male walrus, which may be 50 percent heavier than female*

# Social life

THE SOCIAL LIVES of marine mammals are as varied as the animals themselves. Many seals spend the mating season crowded together on beaches (pp. 28–29). Some whales live alone; others such as the killer whale spend their whole lives in a small group of close relatives (pp. 34–35). Living in a group protects against attack and allows animals to share in the care of young. Many species of whale also hunt in groups, cooperating to round up fish or even attack other whales or seals (pp. 34–35). Planning and executing complex behavior like this takes intelligence, and whales seem to be extremely clever. Whales and dolphins are playful and learn new tasks quickly. But does this make them intelligent? It is hard to judge, because our world is so different from theirs.

**FIGHTING FOR A SPOT**
Good spots for seals and sea lions to come ashore are few and far between. They prefer remote islands and sandbanks, far away from predators such as wolves, bears, or people. So these beaches are crowded with aggressive males and females nursing young pups.

**SWIMMING LESSONS**
Like many young whales, this humpback calf swims close to its mother and is pulled along almost effortlessly in her slipstream. The bond between mother and young is very strong in all mammals. Many whales drink mother's milk for several years. A young whale has a lot to learn. Even taking a breath takes some practice, and newborn whales often bob right out of the water. But with a little help from their mother, they soon learn to surface gracefully.

**FATHER AND SON?**
This Steller's sea lion pup is resting on the back of a huge male, who may be its father. Neither the pup nor the male can know for sure. Because of this uncertainty, male seals have little to do with family life beyond mating with females.

## DANCE OF THE DOLPHINS
Dolphin societies are complex and difficult for people to observe. The warm, shallow waters of the Bahamas are one of the few places in the world where schools can be studied over long periods. These spotted dolphins live in schools of 50 or more. Like other social animals, dolphins have disagreements and conflicts. They often confront each other head to head, squawking with open mouths. These conflicts rarely end in physical injury.

### SUCKLING SEA LION
This female Steller's sea lion is many times smaller than the male below. She is suckling a young pup. The breeding beaches are so crowded that pups are often crushed when the huge males rush over to mate with females. A female leaves her pup regularly to go fishing. So how does she tell her pup from the hundreds of others on the beach when she gets back? She starts by making a warbling call which attracts any nearby pups. Then she smells and touches any likely-looking youngsters until she is sure she has found hers.

## THE DAILY STRUGGLE
These Steller's sea lions are fighting over a fish. During the day, groups of about 50 sea lions have been seen heading out to sea. They work together to find and herd schools of fish or squid.
At night, the sea lions usually hunt alone.

*Female sperm whale rolling upside down*

*Calf*

*Female sperm whale*

*Female rolling upside-down*

### COMMUNAL BABY-SITTING
Because whales live so long, studying their family lives takes decades. Such studies have only just begun, and little is known about most species. We know that female sperm whales live together in big groups with their young calves (p. 39). Males spend only a few hours with each family group every year. One of the females in this group is probably the mother of the small calf. The other females may be sisters or aunts. When the mother dives deep under water to feed, another female will baby-sit the calf, protecting it from sharks or killer whales.

# Dolphins and porpoises

P<small>EOPLE HAVE LONG</small> been fascinated by the graceful dolphin. Imagine the magical sight of a school of dolphins leaping for the sheer fun of it, or bow-wave riding, cruising effortlessly on the pressure waves of a boat. The oceangoing dolphins and their close relatives the porpoises are common in all the world's oceans (except for the coldest polar seas). There is still discussion about how the 60 or more species are related. Some species number in the millions and are found all over the world. Others are limited to tiny areas, which makes them more vulnerable. A few species have been reduced to very low numbers by human activity (pp. 58–59). So far, no species has become extinct, and there may just be time to save the two most at risk, the Gulf of California porpoise (vaquita) and the Chinese river dolphin (p. 63).

**PORPOISING**
Leaping into the air while swimming along is called porpoising. Strangely enough, most porpoises never do it! The one exception is Dall's porpoise.

**LE DAUPHIN**
The eldest son of the king of France was given the title *Le Dauphin*, French for "The Dolphin". The title was first adopted by the lords of Viennois, France, who had three dolphins on their coat of arms. When his father died, *Le Dauphin* became king. What happened to the last *Dauphin*, the son of Louis XVI, is still a mystery. His father was executed in 1793, during the French Revolution.

*Tail flukes with a central nick, like virtually all whales*

**WITH TIME ON HIS SIDE**
Almost nothing is known about the hourglass dolphin, which gets its name from the pretty black-and-white pattern on its sides. Though these dolphins are not shy and often bow-wave ride, they are usually found far out to sea in the remote waters of the southern oceans.

**FISHY TAILS**
The ancient Minoans and Greeks were fascinated by dolphins, which were more common in the Mediterranean Sea at the time those civilizations flourished. Many Greek myths and legends feature dolphins (pp. 54–55). Like most seafarers, Greek sailors were happy to see dolphins playing near their boats. These animals come from the great palace of Knossos on the island of Crete. They are about 3,500 years old. The painter has given the dolphins vertical tails, so they look more like fish.

**ACROBAT**
Dusky dolphins are great leapers. They are coastal animals that live off New Zealand, southern Africa, and South America. Off Peru they are hunted in large numbers for their meat.

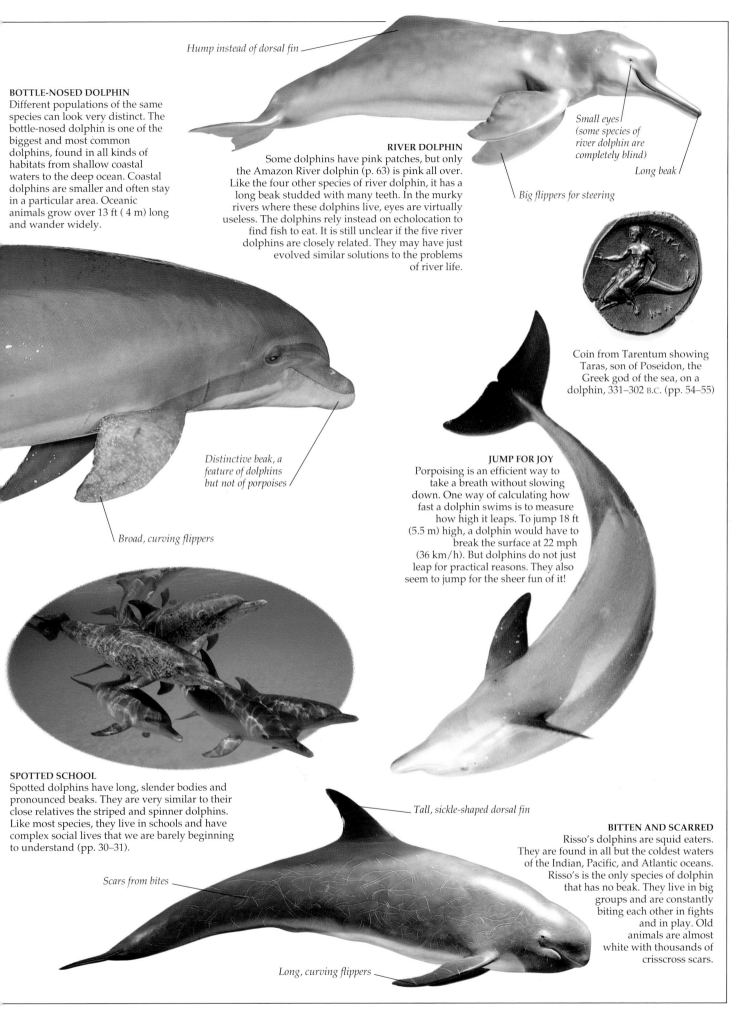

*Hump instead of dorsal fin*

## BOTTLE-NOSED DOLPHIN
Different populations of the same species can look very distinct. The bottle-nosed dolphin is one of the biggest and most common dolphins, found in all kinds of habitats from shallow coastal waters to the deep ocean. Coastal dolphins are smaller and often stay in a particular area. Oceanic animals grow over 13 ft ( 4 m) long and wander widely.

## RIVER DOLPHIN
Some dolphins have pink patches, but only the Amazon River dolphin (p. 63) is pink all over. Like the four other species of river dolphin, it has a long beak studded with many teeth. In the murky rivers where these dolphins live, eyes are virtually useless. The dolphins rely instead on echolocation to find fish to eat. It is still unclear if the five river dolphins are closely related. They may have just evolved similar solutions to the problems of river life.

*Small eyes (some species of river dolphin are completely blind)*

*Long beak*

*Big flippers for steering*

*Distinctive beak, a feature of dolphins but not of porpoises*

*Broad, curving flippers*

Coin from Tarentum showing Taras, son of Poseidon, the Greek god of the sea, on a dolphin, 331–302 B.C. (pp. 54–55)

## JUMP FOR JOY
Porpoising is an efficient way to take a breath without slowing down. One way of calculating how fast a dolphin swims is to measure how high it leaps. To jump 18 ft (5.5 m) high, a dolphin would have to break the surface at 22 mph (36 km/h). But dolphins do not just leap for practical reasons. They also seem to jump for the sheer fun of it!

## SPOTTED SCHOOL
Spotted dolphins have long, slender bodies and pronounced beaks. They are very similar to their close relatives the striped and spinner dolphins. Like most species, they live in schools and have complex social lives that we are barely beginning to understand (pp. 30–31).

*Tall, sickle-shaped dorsal fin*

## BITTEN AND SCARRED
Risso's dolphins are squid eaters. They are found in all but the coldest waters of the Indian, Pacific, and Atlantic oceans. Risso's is the only species of dolphin that has no beak. They live in big groups and are constantly biting each other in fights and in play. Old animals are almost white with thousands of crisscross scars.

*Scars from bites*

*Long, curving flippers*

# The killer whale

**GIANT KILLERS**
Imagine the struggle between a great whale and a pod of killers. Even a huge blue whale has no chance against such an attack. Orcas have been seen organizing attacks on all sorts of whales, including a whole pod of sperm whales.

THERE IS NO MISTAKING an orca, or killer whale, with its tall dorsal fin, rounded head and startling black-and-white pattern. An adult male can be 30 ft (9 m) long and weigh 11 tons (10 tonnes). Most of this is muscle, for the orca is the fastest mammal in the seas (p. 19), sprinting at up to 34 mph (56 km/h). This awesome hunter eats almost everything, from small fish to great whales 10 times its size. Because of its ferocious appetite, the orca's common name is killer whale. Orcas have no natural predators. Until the 1960s, they were feared and sometimes shot. But opinions have changed, partly because orcas do not seem to eat humans. Orcas live long lives – a female may reach 90 years old. But they reproduce slowly, with a calf about every eight years. They live in tight social groups called pods, hunt cooperatively, and seem to be highly intelligent. Pods of orcas have been seen working together to herd salmon or tip a seal off an ice floe.

**FALSE KILLER**
Like the two kinds of pilot whale, this false killer whale is a close relative of the orca. False killers are black all over. They swim with a slow, lazy action. They are the largest whales to bow-wave ride, hitching a free swim from the waves made by boats (p. 32). False killers occasionally eat other marine mammals.

Eye

White patch, not eye!

Stiff dorsal fin

Rounded flippers are black top and bottom

White belly

**WHY ARE THEY BLACK AND WHITE?**
The jet black and shocking white may help to camouflage a killer whale by breaking up its outline. This makes it hard to see as it flits through the water.

**SURPRISE!**
Orcas are one of the few whales that come onto shore, on purpose (pp. 56–57). On the Valdés Peninsula in Argentina and the Crozet Islands in the Indian Ocean, orcas swim up onto the beach to grab baby sea lions. Then they use their front flippers to turn around and wiggle back into the surf while they hold the sea lion firmly in their jaws.

**LIKE A CAT WITH A MOUSE**
All is not yet over for the sea lion. The orca plays with the limp animal like a cat with a mouse. It will fling its prey high into the air with a quick flick of the tail. Young orcas have to learn how to do this, and often join their parents in the game. Finally the terrified sea lion is eaten.

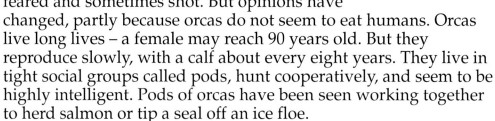

**PEA IN A POD**
This female killer
is only seven years old and already weighs 2.2 tons
(2 tonnes). Both males and females remain in the same
pod as their mother for life. An older female seems to be
in charge of the pod. Orcas never mate within a pod, but
only when two pods meet. They breach and lobtail a lot
during these exciting encounters.

**IT'S A FAMILY AFFAIR**
This orca pod lives in British Columbia, Canada. They belong to
the best-studied population of whales anywhere in the world.
The 200-plus individuals are easily recognized by the nicks in
their dorsal fins (p. 60) and the shapes of their "saddles," the
gray patches behind the fins. The mature male in this pod has a
huge dorsal fin. These fins can grow to be 6 ft (2 m) tall.

*Melon*

**SHOULD I STAY OR SHOULD I GO?**
Orcas live in every ocean of the world. Researchers in
British Columbia have found two types. Resident
orcas stay in one area, where they eat fish
and squid and make a lot of underwater sounds. In contrast, transients
(wanderers) roam widely. They
move stealthily and silently
and tackle larger prey
like seals and other
whales.

*Blowhole*

**BIG SUCKERS**
Fishermen and orcas are often in
conflict. In many areas, the fishermen feel that orcas eat valuable
salmon and herring. The whales
are clever. In Alaska, orcas follow
fishing boats and gently suck the
fish from the lines as they are
hauled in. The fishermen pull
up nothing but the
fishes' lips.

# The amazing narwhal

THE MYTHICAL UNICORN, a white horse with a horn growing out of its forehead, was really a whale – the "unicorn-whale" or narwhal. Narwhal tusks were sold in Europe long before the real animal was widely known, so it was easy for imaginative traders to claim that the tusks came from unicorns. Even today the narwhal is a mysterious animal. We are still not certain what its strange overgrown tooth is for, though people have offered many ideas. Like its close relative the beluga, the narwhal lives in the remote, icy waters of the Arctic and so is hard to study. Both narwhals and belugas migrate with the seasons, following the receding ice north in the summer and south in the winter. As the sea freezes over, they are sometimes trapped in the ice. They can usually keep breathing holes open, but many narwhals and belugas probably drown when the ice catches them far from open water.

**THE UNICORN**
In the Middle Ages, narwhal tusks were sold as unicorn horns, which were thought to have magical properties. Cups made from them were supposed to neutralize any poison. The tusks were also ground into a medicinal powder. This was still sold in Japan in the 1950s under the name *ikkaku*.

*Row of low bumps instead of dorsal fin*

*Fan-shaped tail, more marked in older narwhals*

*Right tooth, which usually does not grow beyond the gums*

*Pectoral flipper*

*Left tooth, or tusk, grows in a counterclockwise spiral*

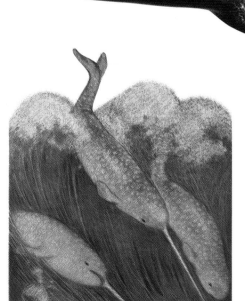

**WHAT'S IT FOR?**
People have suggested all kinds of uses for the narwhal's tusk. Some guess that the giant tooth is used to spear fish or to break holes in the ice. Others say the narwhal may use it as a hoe to root out animals on the ocean floor. But all these ideas are probably wrong, because they do not explain why males have tusks, while females survive very well without them!

**LONG IN THE TOOTH**
A bottom view of a male narwhal's skull shows the roots of its mighty tooth. All narwhals have two teeth, though in females they almost never grow beyond the gums. The same is usually true for a male's right tooth, while the left grows out to become the tusk. In adults, the tusk can be 10 ft (3 m), more than half as long as the whale's body. Every now and then a female grows a tusk, or a male grows two. Two-tusked skulls were especially prized, and many are displayed in museums.

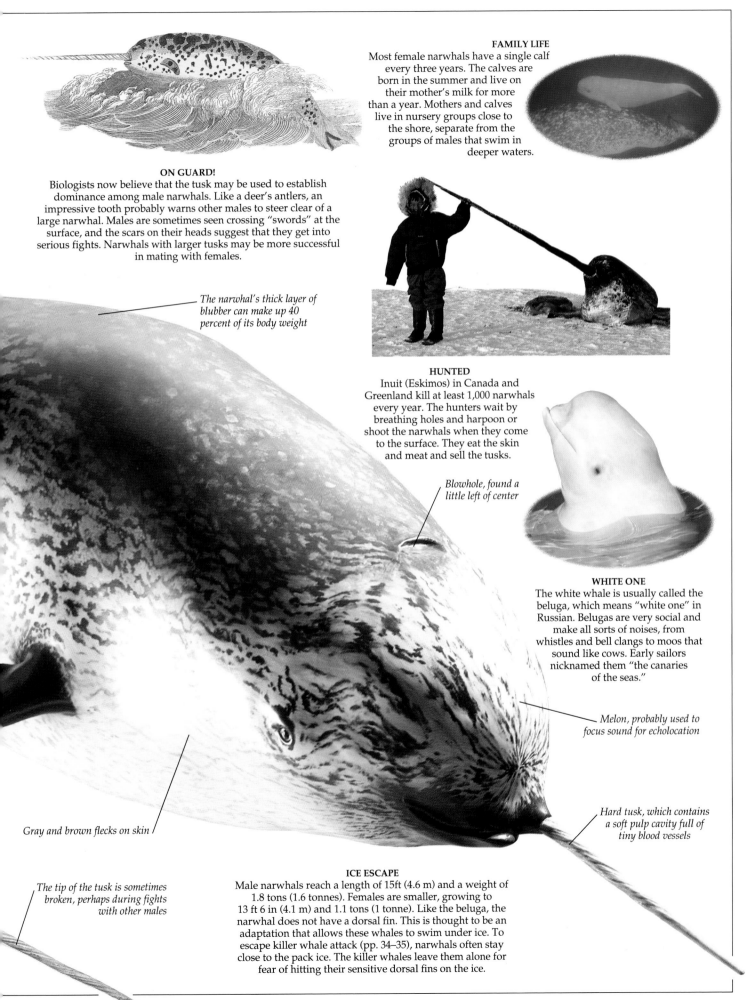

**FAMILY LIFE**
Most female narwhals have a single calf every three years. The calves are born in the summer and live on their mother's milk for more than a year. Mothers and calves live in nursery groups close to the shore, separate from the groups of males that swim in deeper waters.

**ON GUARD!**
Biologists now believe that the tusk may be used to establish dominance among male narwhals. Like a deer's antlers, an impressive tooth probably warns other males to steer clear of a large narwhal. Males are sometimes seen crossing "swords" at the surface, and the scars on their heads suggest that they get into serious fights. Narwhals with larger tusks may be more successful in mating with females.

*The narwhal's thick layer of blubber can make up 40 percent of its body weight*

**HUNTED**
Inuit (Eskimos) in Canada and Greenland kill at least 1,000 narwhals every year. The hunters wait by breathing holes and harpoon or shoot the narwhals when they come to the surface. They eat the skin and meat and sell the tusks.

*Blowhole, found a little left of center*

**WHITE ONE**
The white whale is usually called the beluga, which means "white one" in Russian. Belugas are very social and make all sorts of noises, from whistles and bell clangs to moos that sound like cows. Early sailors nicknamed them "the canaries of the seas."

*Melon, probably used to focus sound for echolocation*

*Gray and brown flecks on skin*

*Hard tusk, which contains a soft pulp cavity full of tiny blood vessels*

*The tip of the tusk is sometimes broken, perhaps during fights with other males*

**ICE ESCAPE**
Male narwhals reach a length of 15ft (4.6 m) and a weight of 1.8 tons (1.6 tonnes). Females are smaller, growing to 13 ft 6 in (4.1 m) and 1.1 tons (1 tonne). Like the beluga, the narwhal does not have a dorsal fin. This is thought to be an adaptation that allows these whales to swim under ice. To escape killer whale attack (pp. 34–35), narwhals often stay close to the pack ice. The killer whales leave them alone for fear of hitting their sensitive dorsal fins on the ice.

# The sperm whale

SPERM WHALES HAVE THE LARGEST brains that have ever existed and a range that spans the globe. They are creatures of the open ocean that dive to incredible depths to feed on squid, a food resource that is out of reach of most other predators. A male sperm whale eats more than a ton of squid a day, and every year sperm whales eat more food than the total amount caught by all the world's fishermen. We still know little about how the whale hunts in its dark underwater world. The function of its huge square forehead is also unclear. It may help the sperm whale dive to such amazing depths. The whale may even use its head to produce powerful clicks to stun its prey.

_Sperm whale rib_

**MADEIRA SPERM WHALE**
Catching sperm whales from open boats was a dangerous occupation (pp. 46–47). Until a few years ago, whales were still killed in this way off Madeira and the Azores Islands in the Atlantic Ocean. The Azores population is still healthy, but there are few sperm whales left off Madeira.

**THE WHITE WHALE**
The most famous sperm whale is Moby Dick, the hero of Herman Melville's novel. It is the story of Captain Ahab, who has lost a leg in a battle with the huge white whale. He becomes obsessed with killing the whale and hunts it all over the globe. In the end, Moby Dick sinks the ship and the captain goes down with it. Albino (white) sperm whales do occur, but they are very rare.

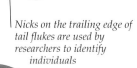

_Nicks on the trailing edge of tail flukes are used by researchers to identify individuals_

**PYGMY SPERM**
Almost nothing is known about the pygmy and dwarf sperm whales, the other members of the family. Both are relatively small, less than 10 ft (3 m) long. Like the sperm whale, they are deep divers that live in the open ocean.

**FOUL-SMELLING PEARL**
Once worth its weight in gold, ambergris is a foul-smelling wax that was used to make perfumes. It is occasionally secreted in the sperm whale's guts, perhaps around squid beaks. Whalers who found a lump of ambergris considered it a valuable prize. It sometimes washes ashore in places such as the Maldive Islands, to the delight of the local people.

**GIANT SQUID**
Only one man, a whaler by the name of Frank Bullen, has ever seen a battle between a giant squid and a sperm whale. The largest squid ever found in a whale's stomach was 39 ft (12 m) long! But the average size is much smaller, and even monster squid must have little chance against a sperm whale. The famous "battles" are probably just the squids wriggling to try and get out of the whale's jaws.

**MAKING A SPLASH**
This sperm whale is lobtailing – lifting its muscular tail flukes into the air and slamming them down on the water. Like breaching (p. 27), this is probably a way of communicating. It is usually females that lobtail, often in the presence of males. The big splashes made by lobtailing and breaching can be heard a long distance under water.

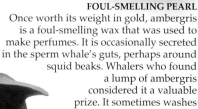

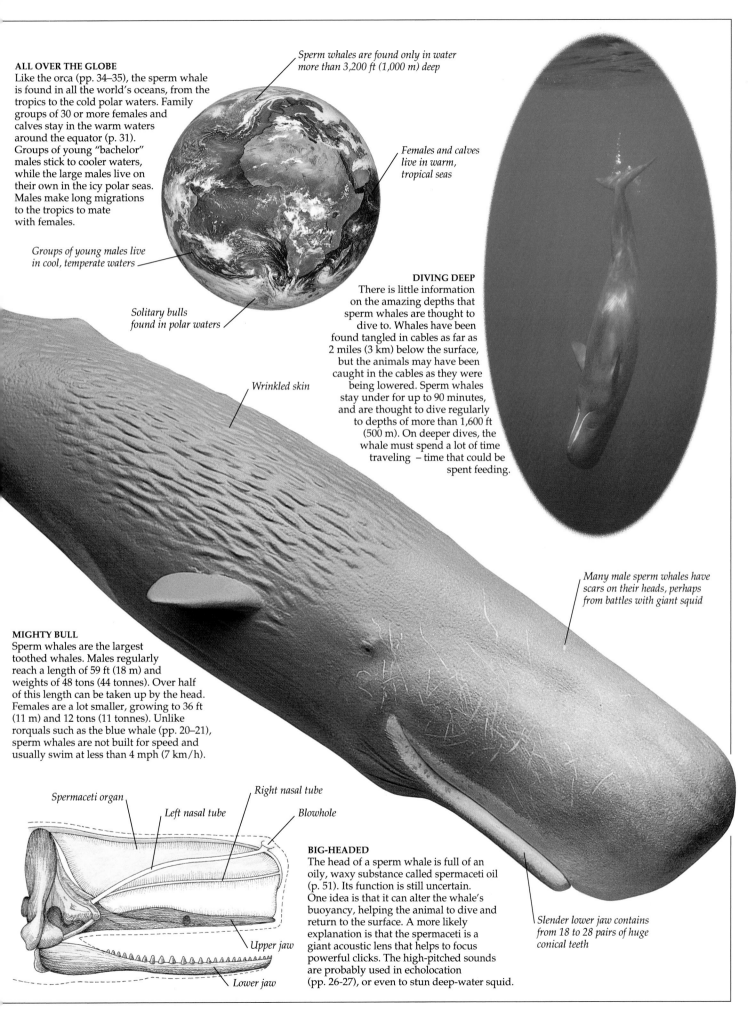

## ALL OVER THE GLOBE

Like the orca (pp. 34–35), the sperm whale is found in all the world's oceans, from the tropics to the cold polar waters. Family groups of 30 or more females and calves stay in the warm waters around the equator (p. 31). Groups of young "bachelor" males stick to cooler waters, while the large males live on their own in the icy polar seas. Males make long migrations to the tropics to mate with females.

*Sperm whales are found only in water more than 3,200 ft (1,000 m) deep*

*Females and calves live in warm, tropical seas*

*Groups of young males live in cool, temperate waters*

*Solitary bulls found in polar waters*

*Wrinkled skin*

## DIVING DEEP

There is little information on the amazing depths that sperm whales are thought to dive to. Whales have been found tangled in cables as far as 2 miles (3 km) below the surface, but the animals may have been caught in the cables as they were being lowered. Sperm whales stay under for up to 90 minutes, and are thought to dive regularly to depths of more than 1,600 ft (500 m). On deeper dives, the whale must spend a lot of time traveling – time that could be spent feeding.

*Many male sperm whales have scars on their heads, perhaps from battles with giant squid*

## MIGHTY BULL

Sperm whales are the largest toothed whales. Males regularly reach a length of 59 ft (18 m) and weights of 48 tons (44 tonnes). Over half of this length can be taken up by the head. Females are a lot smaller, growing to 36 ft (11 m) and 12 tons (11 tonnes). Unlike rorquals such as the blue whale (pp. 20–21), sperm whales are not built for speed and usually swim at less than 4 mph (7 km/h).

*Spermaceti organ*

*Left nasal tube*

*Right nasal tube*

*Blowhole*

## BIG-HEADED

The head of a sperm whale is full of an oily, waxy substance called spermaceti oil (p. 51). Its function is still uncertain. One idea is that it can alter the whale's buoyancy, helping the animal to dive and return to the surface. A more likely explanation is that the spermaceti is a giant acoustic lens that helps to focus powerful clicks. The high-pitched sounds are probably used in echolocation (pp. 26-27), or even to stun deep-water squid.

*Upper jaw*

*Lower jaw*

*Slender lower jaw contains from 18 to 28 pairs of huge conical teeth*

# The elephant seal

## WHAT A SCHNOZZ!
Male elephants seals are up to 10 times heavier than females (which do not have such large noses). Every male tries to control a harem (group) of females and keep other males away. He scares off rivals by bellowing, rearing up on his belly, and filling his nose with air. He hopes that other males will think he is huge and leave him in peace.

## BATTLE OF THE GIANTS
These two males are fighting for control of a beach crowded with females. These battles start with a lot of huffing and puffing and showing off of noses. Usually the smaller male then sneaks away and avoids a fight. But two big males may have a violent showdown. Most large males are covered with scars and bite marks.

THE ELEPHANT seal gets its name from the male's huge, swollen nose, which plays an important role in the seal's mating ritual. Elephant seals are enormous, weighing up to 3.3 tons (three tonnes). They come ashore in large groups to mate, give birth, and suckle their young. There is constant activity on the crowded beaches as the biggest, strongest males battle for places among the females, while less dominant males hang around the edges. The pups and females grunt and groan, and the males roar. These beaches are dangerous places for people, who could be attacked by an aggressive male. There are two species of elephant seal, southern and northern. Although they live thousands of miles apart, they are thought to be closely related. Northern elephant seals are found off the west coast of North America, where they haul out (come ashore) on isolated islands from San Francisco to Baja, Mexico. Southern elephant seals are found all around the Antarctic.

## NOSE JOB
Most animals just use their noses to smell. But the elephant's trunk is like an arm, good for picking up objects, even spraying water like a hose. The sperm whale has the largest nose of all. It probably uses this to focus sounds (p. 38–39).

*The elephant seal is a true seal and cannot tuck its hind flippers under its body*

## BLUBBERING ABOUT
Elephant seals are deep divers. They are known to reach depths of more than a half-mile below the surface (p. 61). At such depths the pressure is enormous. A fur coat would not keep the animal warm, because the bubbles trapped between the hairs would be compressed to almost nothing (p. 16). Instead, elephant seals stay warm with thick layers of blubber.

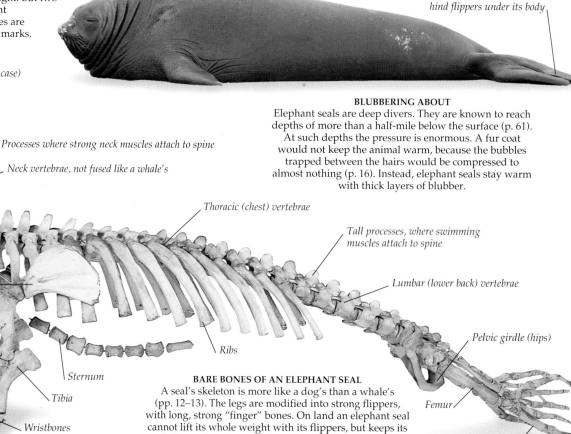

Cranium (brain case)

Processes where strong neck muscles attach to spine

Neck vertebrae, not fused like a whale's

Massive lower jaw

Clavicle (collarbone)

Scapula (shoulder blade)

Humerus

Thoracic (chest) vertebrae

Tall processes, where swimming muscles attach to spine

Lumbar (lower back) vertebrae

Fibia

Sternum

Tibia

Ribs

Pelvic girdle (hips)

Phalanges (finger bones)

Wristbones

Femur

Phalanges (toe bones)

## BARE BONES OF AN ELEPHANT SEAL
A seal's skeleton is more like a dog's than a whale's (pp. 12–13). The legs are modified into strong flippers, with long, strong "finger" bones. On land an elephant seal cannot lift its whole weight with its flippers, but keeps its belly on the ground and moves by flexing its back.

### TRUE LOVE?
The female elephant
seal (on the left) cannot really say no when
it comes to mating. The huge male pins her
down and may bite her neck to keep her
still. As soon as he finishes, he moves on to
the next female.

### MILK LIKE MAYONNAISE
Seal milk looks like mayonnaise.
Southern elephant seal milk contains up
to 43 percent fat. The mother does not
eat at all for the whole three to four
weeks of suckling. She loses a lot of
weight, while the pup puts it on fast.
Some northern elephant seal pups grow
even faster by sneaking milk from
several females.

*Half of body weight
may be blubber*

*Large front flippers,
used to steer while
swimming*

### POLLUTED BEACH
A big threat to elephant seals these days is
pollution. Most of this ugly rubbish is
harmless. But seals often get tangled in
packing straps and nets. As the seal
grows, its neck or flipper is cut by the
hard plastic. This is a slow and painful
way to die.

### WE ARE FAMILY
The northern elephant seal was
hunted almost to extinction at the
end of the 19th century (pp. 52–53).
When the killing stopped, there
were less than 100 seals left. This
small band of survivors made an
incredible recovery, and all the
animals of this species that are
alive today are descended
from them. The population
has reached 120,000. But all
these seals are closely
related, and people are
worried that they may
suffer from inbreeding.

*Hind flippers, the seal's
driving force*

# I am the walrus

**TRADITIONAL FOOD SOURCE**
The Inuit still kill walruses, as they always have. But in the last three centuries, Europeans hunted large numbers commercially (pp. 52–53). The herds suffered greatly, and only the North Pacific population has completely recovered.

WITH ITS HUGE TUSKS, bushy mustache, and thick rolls of blubber, the walrus is unlike any other seal. For this reason it is put in a family all its own. There are about 250,000 walruses left, all found in the cold waters of the North Pacific and Atlantic oceans. They live in large groups which huddle together for warmth. The life cycle of the walrus follows the seasonal ebb and flow of the Arctic ice. Females give birth in spring. Then they migrate as far as 1,800 miles (3,000 km) north following the melting ice. Despite their huge size, walruses have two formidable enemies: polar bears (p. 7) and killer whales. In the Canadian Arctic, bears are seen chasing or sneaking up on walruses. In Russia, polar bears have even been seen throwing chunks of ice at them! A pod of killer whales (pp. 34–35) hunts together, rounding up the walruses and taking turns swimming through the middle of the herd with their jaws open wide. They may also ram ice floes to try to tip walruses into the sea.

**TOOTH WALK**
The German artist Albrecht Dürer drew a walrus pulling itself onto an ice floe with its tusks. This explains the Latin name, *Odobenus rosmarus*, which means "tooth-walking seahorse." Tusks are also useful for enlarging breathing holes in the ice.

**THE TIME HAS COME, THE WALRUS SAID...**
Lewis Carroll's famous story *Through the Looking-Glass* stars a walrus and a carpenter. They invite some oysters to take a walk with them. As you might have guessed, the oysters end up being eaten! In real life, walruses do eat shellfish, but they stick to bivalves like clams that live in the mud (p. 23). They spit jets of water into the murky sea floor to help root out their food.

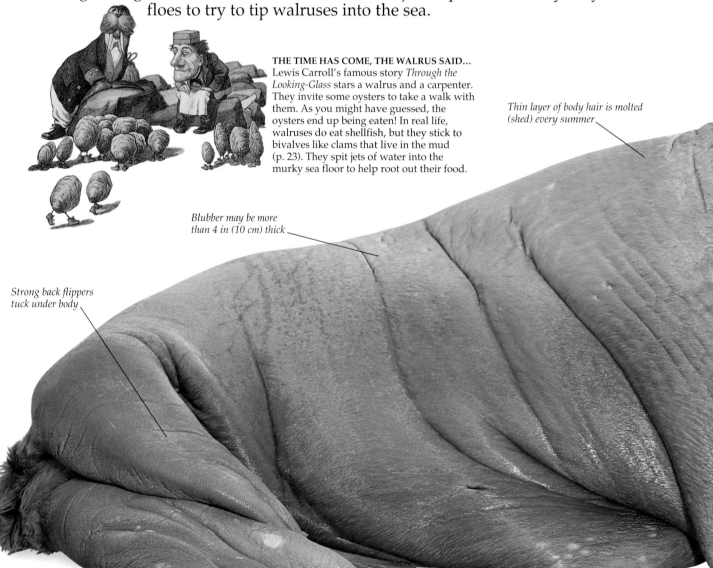

*Thin layer of body hair is molted (shed) every summer*

*Blubber may be more than 4 in (10 cm) thick*

*Strong back flippers tuck under body*

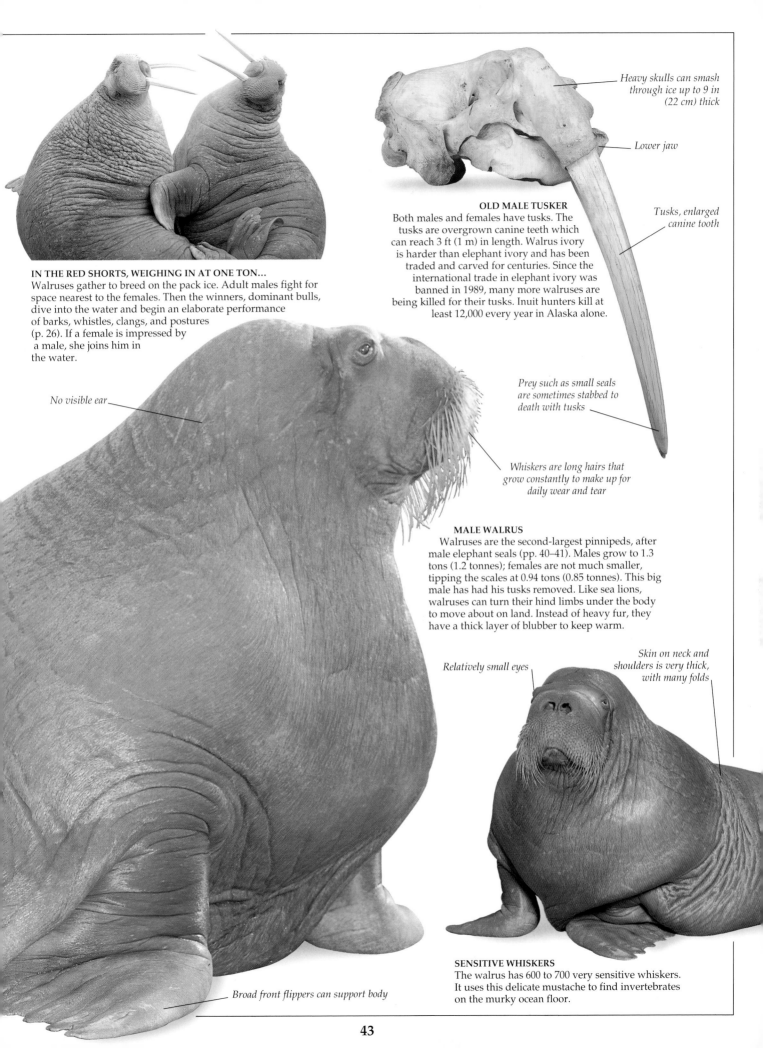

**IN THE RED SHORTS, WEIGHING IN AT ONE TON...**
Walruses gather to breed on the pack ice. Adult males fight for
space nearest to the females. Then the winners, dominant bulls,
dive into the water and begin an elaborate performance
of barks, whistles, clangs, and postures
(p. 26). If a female is impressed by
a male, she joins him in
the water.

Heavy skulls can smash
through ice up to 9 in
(22 cm) thick

Lower jaw

**OLD MALE TUSKER**
Both males and females have tusks. The
tusks are overgrown canine teeth which
can reach 3 ft (1 m) in length. Walrus ivory
is harder than elephant ivory and has been
traded and carved for centuries. Since the
international trade in elephant ivory was
banned in 1989, many more walruses are
being killed for their tusks. Inuit hunters kill at
least 12,000 every year in Alaska alone.

Tusks, enlarged
canine tooth

No visible ear

Prey such as small seals
are sometimes stabbed to
death with tusks

Whiskers are long hairs that
grow constantly to make up for
daily wear and tear

**MALE WALRUS**
Walruses are the second-largest pinnipeds, after
male elephant seals (pp. 40–41). Males grow to 1.3
tons (1.2 tonnes); females are not much smaller,
tipping the scales at 0.94 tons (0.85 tonnes). This big
male has had his tusks removed. Like sea lions,
walruses can turn their hind limbs under the body
to move about on land. Instead of heavy fur, they
have a thick layer of blubber to keep warm.

Skin on neck and
shoulders is very thick,
with many folds

Relatively small eyes

Broad front flippers can support body

**SENSITIVE WHISKERS**
The walrus has 600 to 700 very sensitive whiskers.
It uses this delicate mustache to find invertebrates
on the murky ocean floor.

43

# Sea cows

WITH THEIR FLESHY SNOUTS, chubby bodies, and gentle ways, dugongs and manatees are, not surprisingly, often called sea cows. The three species of manatee and the single species of dugong all live in warm waters. They are slow-moving vegetarians, grazing on sea grass, water hyacinths, and occasionally seaweed. Manatees stay in rivers or salty estuaries and rarely venture into the open sea. This makes the dugong the only vegetarian marine (sea-going) mammal. Like whales, manatees and dugongs have lost their back legs and spend their entire lives in the water. Also like whales, they reproduce slowly, giving birth to one calf every three years. Therefore they are very vulnerable to extinction. Wherever they occur, dugongs are hunted for their tasty meat. Many manatees and dugongs are also killed in collisions with boats.

**MERMAID**
Since ancient times, sailors have told stories of mermaids, beautiful women with fishes' tails. The legends are probably based on sightings of dugongs or manatees. But you would have to spend a long time at sea to imagine a dugong was a beautiful woman! Mermaids were bad omens and were said to lure ships onto rocks.

**WEST INDIAN MANATEE**
The West Indian manatee has been studied more than its relatives. Weighing up to 1.7 tons (1.6 tonnes), this fat vegetarian lives in coastal waters, estuaries, and rivers in parts of the Caribbean and Atlantic. Adult males travel widely and often gather in large groups around females that are ready to mate. Manatees can stay under water for 10 to 15 minutes and digest their food slowly in their long guts.

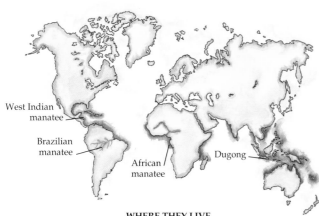

West Indian manatee

Brazilian manatee

African manatee

Dugong

**WHERE THEY LIVE**
Of the three species of manatee, one never leaves the Amazon River, and the other two live in estuaries as well as rivers. The dugong is entirely marine.

**NOISY EATERS**
Manatees and dugongs are specialized eaters, the only mammals that feed on underwater vegetation. Manatees are noisy eaters. When they feed at the surface, the chomping of their teeth and flapping of their lips are easy to hear. Semi-captive manatees have even been used as underwater lawn mowers, to clear waterways and dams choked with water hyacinths. In the sea, they eat varieties of sea grass.

**POWER HUNGRY**
This manatee has algae growing all over its back. If manatees get too cold, they become constipated and die. So in winter, they seek out warm waters such as hot springs. In Florida, manatees gather around the warm water outlets of power stations and factories. This may endanger their long-term health.

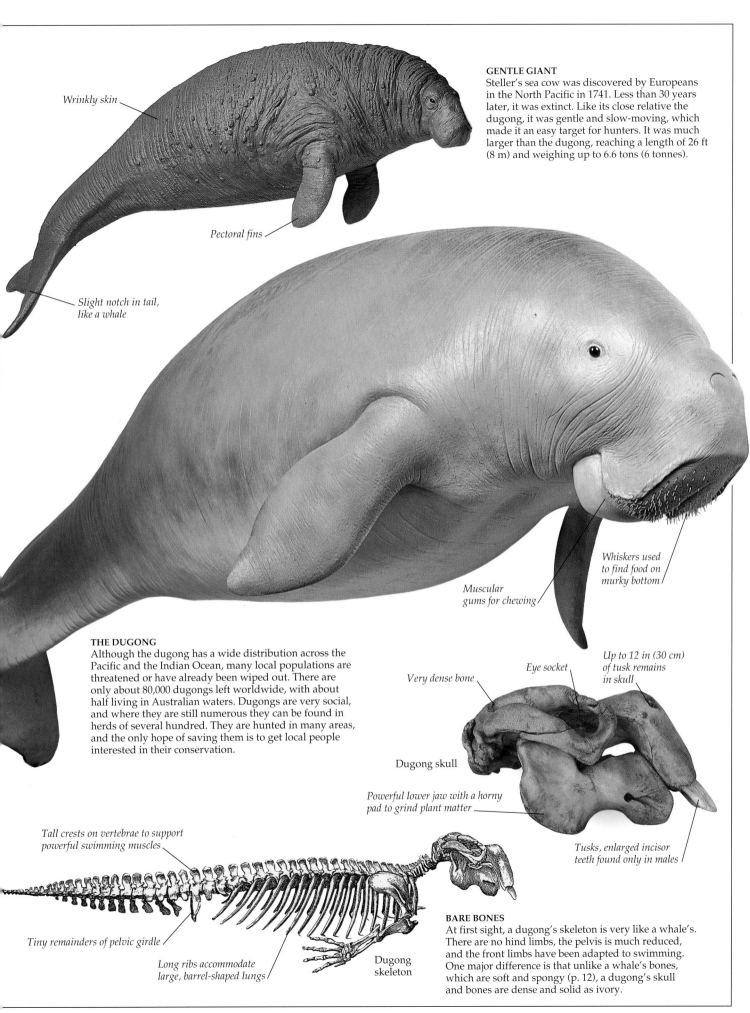

_Wrinkly skin_

**GENTLE GIANT**
Steller's sea cow was discovered by Europeans in the North Pacific in 1741. Less than 30 years later, it was extinct. Like its close relative the dugong, it was gentle and slow-moving, which made it an easy target for hunters. It was much larger than the dugong, reaching a length of 26 ft (8 m) and weighing up to 6.6 tons (6 tonnes).

_Pectoral fins_

_Slight notch in tail, like a whale_

_Whiskers used to find food on murky bottom_

_Muscular gums for chewing_

**THE DUGONG**
Although the dugong has a wide distribution across the Pacific and the Indian Ocean, many local populations are threatened or have already been wiped out. There are only about 80,000 dugongs left worldwide, with about half living in Australian waters. Dugongs are very social, and where they are still numerous they can be found in herds of several hundred. They are hunted in many areas, and the only hope of saving them is to get local people interested in their conservation.

_Very dense bone_

_Eye socket_

_Up to 12 in (30 cm) of tusk remains in skull_

Dugong skull

_Powerful lower jaw with a horny pad to grind plant matter_

_Tusks, enlarged incisor teeth found only in males_

_Tall crests on vertebrae to support powerful swimming muscles_

_Tiny remainders of pelvic girdle_

_Long ribs accommodate large, barrel-shaped lungs_

Dugong skeleton

**BARE BONES**
At first sight, a dugong's skeleton is very like a whale's. There are no hind limbs, the pelvis is much reduced, and the front limbs have been adapted to swimming. One major difference is that unlike a whale's bones, which are soft and spongy (p. 12), a dugong's skull and bones are dense and solid as ivory.

# Hunting the mighty whale

PEOPLE HAVE HUNTED WHALES for two thousand years. For early whalers like the Vikings, the whale was a sea monster to be conquered in a desperate battle. In the last century, whaling was a dangerous occupation. Ships set sail for the frozen and uncharted Arctic. When a whale was seen, tiny boats were lowered and rowed silently up to the unsuspecting giant. Hand harpoons were thrown into the whale. In the struggle, boats were often overturned and men drowned. Even in those early days far too many whales were killed, and the whalers had to move from place to place to find new stocks (populations) to hunt. Soon large American ships were sailing the world in search of whales.

**YANKEE WHALING BOAT**
When the lookout saw a whale spouting, he let out the traditional cry "Thar she blows!" Then boats were lowered and the whale was harpooned. This model of a Yankee whaling boat is made from sperm whale bones. In the Arctic, the whale was towed ashore to be cut up and boiled down for its oil. But sperm whales are creatures of the open ocean (pp. 38–39), and whalers had to process them aboard ship.

**WHALE OF A POT**
Blubber pots were mounted in pairs on the ship's deck. They were filled with blubber, and a fire was lit below to extract the oil. This was ladled off, cooled, and poured into storage casks.

**KEEPING A GRIP**
Keeping your footing on a whale's slippery back was no easy task. So the whalers who flensed (cut up) the whale wore sharp spurs on their boots, like the crampons used by mountaineers.

**A WHALER'S TOOLS**
Whalers took a variety of tools on their long voyages. Harpoons were thrown from a distance. They were attached to a coil of rope which played out as the whale dived. When the injured, exhausted whale came up for the last time, it was killed with a lance from close quarters. The dead whale was then cut up with various flensing tools.

**BENT IN BATTLE**
Harpoons were made of soft iron, so they could be straightened if they were bent by the whale.

*Bowsprit*

*Lance, used to kill whale*

*Dolphin striker, which holds down bowsprit*

Blubber knife, for cutting through thick layers of fat

Flensing spade, for peeling back rolls of blubber

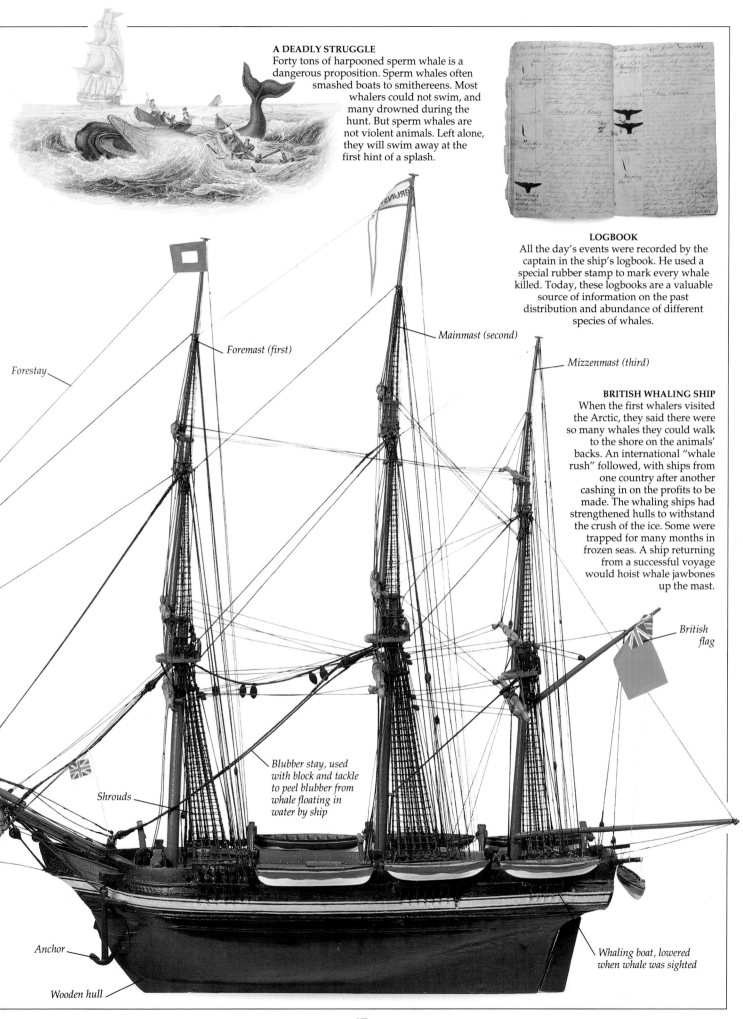

**A DEADLY STRUGGLE**
Forty tons of harpooned sperm whale is a dangerous proposition. Sperm whales often smashed boats to smithereens. Most whalers could not swim, and many drowned during the hunt. But sperm whales are not violent animals. Left alone, they will swim away at the first hint of a splash.

**LOGBOOK**
All the day's events were recorded by the captain in the ship's logbook. He used a special rubber stamp to mark every whale killed. Today, these logbooks are a valuable source of information on the past distribution and abundance of different species of whales.

*Foremast (first)*

*Mainmast (second)*

*Forestay*

*Mizzenmast (third)*

**BRITISH WHALING SHIP**
When the first whalers visited the Arctic, they said there were so many whales they could walk to the shore on the animals' backs. An international "whale rush" followed, with ships from one country after another cashing in on the profits to be made. The whaling ships had strengthened hulls to withstand the crush of the ice. Some were trapped for many months in frozen seas. A ship returning from a successful voyage would hoist whale jawbones up the mast.

*British flag*

*Blubber stay, used with block and tackle to peel blubber from whale floating in water by ship*

*Shrouds*

*Anchor*

*Whaling boat, lowered when whale was sighted*

*Wooden hull*

# Whaling in the 20th century

STEAM-POWERED SHIPS and explosive harpoons revolutionized whaling. With these advances, whalers could hunt the fast rorquals such as fin whales and the mighty blue (pp. 20–21). No animal was safe. The whalers traveled the world, slaughtering population after population. By the turn of the century, they had arrived in the remote, inhospitable waters of the Antarctic. At first the whalers towed dead whales back to shore stations on islands such as South Georgia. Then factory ships that could process dead whales at sea one after another were built . By 1988, a worldwide moratorium (ban) finally brought a pause in commercial whaling. By then, the whalers were under a lot of pressure from conservationists. But the main reason most countries stopped was economic – there were not enough whales left!

**WHAT A FLUKE!**
A whaler is dwarfed by a sperm whale's tail fluke. Since 1946, whaling has been regulated by the International Whaling Commission (IWC). This began as a whaler's club that tried to control the price of whale oil. But now the IWC is looking very carefully at ways to protect the future of whales. It banned the commercial whaling of sperm whales after 1984.

**HITTING THE WHALE**
It is virtually impossible to kill a whale humanely. The vital organs are hard to hit from a moving vessel. Often the harpoons do not explode. Most whales are killed within a few minutes, but some struggle in agony for more than half an hour.

*Tip loaded with grenade which explodes inside whale*

*Barbs open on impact so harpoon is embedded in flesh*

**FLENSING A BLUE**
Before whaling started in the Antarctic, there were about 250,000 blue whales there. Now there may only be a few hundred left. This dead giant was 90 ft (27.4 m) long. The next species to be hunted was the smaller fin whale. Once they became hard to find, the whalers moved on to even smaller sei whales.

**HARPOONING DOLPHINS**
This whaler is harpooning dolphins that have come to bow-wave ride on his boat (p. 32). Even today, there are few restrictions on the hunting of small whales, which are not covered by the IWC. In many countries, dolphins and porpoises are killed for food, sport, or even crab bait.

### THE BOWHEAD HUNT
The Inuit have hunted small numbers of bowhead whales for many centuries. But because of European whaling, the bowhead is now on the verge of extinction (p. 63). These Inuit whalers are flensing (cutting up) a dead whale. They still kill a few bowheads every year. This is not considered a commercial hunt, because no part of the whale is sold.

### THAR SHE BLEEDS
Until very recently, sperm whales were caught off the Atlantic islands of the Azores and Madeira (p. 38). The whalers used small *canoas* (sailing canoes) and hand harpoons, like the Yankee whalers of last century. They towed the dead whales back to stations on shore to be processed. The Azoreans caught several hundred sperm whales each year with these primitive methods.

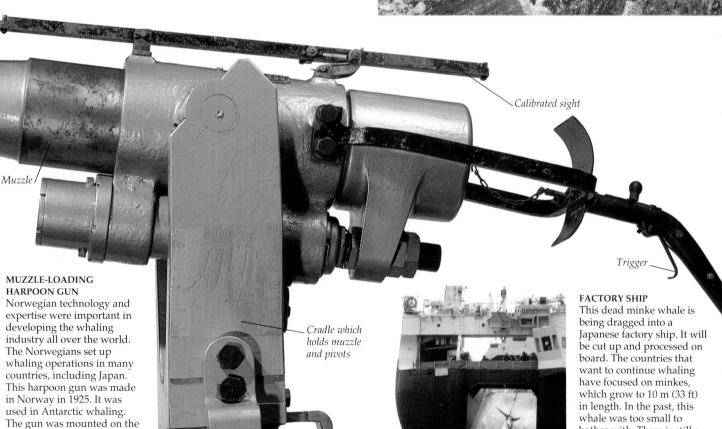

*Calibrated sight*

*Muzzle*

*Trigger*

*Cradle which holds muzzle and pivots*

### MUZZLE-LOADING HARPOON GUN
Norwegian technology and expertise were important in developing the whaling industry all over the world. The Norwegians set up whaling operations in many countries, including Japan. This harpoon gun was made in Norway in 1925. It was used in Antarctic whaling. The gun was mounted on the bow of a boat and loaded with a harpoon with an explosive tip. It was solidly made to absorb the recoil, and accurately balanced so it was easy to aim.

### FACTORY SHIP
This dead minke whale is being dragged into a Japanese factory ship. It will be cut up and processed on board. The countries that want to continue whaling have focused on minkes, which grow to 10 m (33 ft) in length. In the past, this whale was too small to bother with. There is still a considerable number of minkes in the southern oceans, but whaling in the north may have reduced some populations by more than half.

# Oils, brushes, and corsets

THE EARLY WHALERS SUFFERED incredible hardships so the world could have brushes, oil, soap, candles, umbrellas, and corsets. In an age before petroleum or plastics, whales provided valuable raw materials for thousands of everyday objects. Right whales were killed for their oil and baleen (pp. 24–25). The oil was refined and sold to be burned in lamps. Baleen, often given the misleading name "whalebone," was a tough, springy material used to stiffen corsets and as bristles for brushes. Sperm whales were hunted for the oil in their heads. At first this was burned in lamps and used to make candles. As the machine age unfolded, sperm oil became a high-grade lubricant for motors and cars. The whaling of other species ended because there were not enough whales left. But sperm whaling ended with the discovery of petroleum, a cheaper source of oil. Nowadays, alternatives have been found for all whale products. But whale meat has become a gourmet food item in Japan, where it can sell for $80 a pound.

**TIGHT FIT**
Women wore very uncomfortable clothes years ago. They were squeezed into elaborate corsets stiffened with baleen ("whalebone").

Necklace made from whale bone

**PILLS AND SOAP**
Like all oils, whale oil can be turned into soap through a simple chemical process. Early in the 20th century, foods such as margarine and ice cream were also made from whale oil.

**SCRAPING A LIVING**
Many whale-related industries were set up in whaling ports. Here baleen from right whales is being scraped clean before being manufactured into the various products on these pages. Two whaling ships can be seen in the port in the background.

Chimney sweep's brush with baleen bristles

Floor brush with baleen bristles

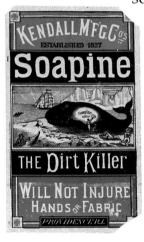

**BALEEN BRUSHES**
These days most brushes are made from plastics. But a hundred years ago, baleen was shredded to make brush bristles.

Comb made from baleen

Hairbrush with baleen bristles

### SCRIMSHAW

On whalers' long voyages, they passed the time decorating whales' teeth and bones. This engraving is called scrimshaw. The designs were made more visible by rubbing soot into the scratches.

### BURNING BRIGHT

What a live sperm whale does with the quarts of oil in its huge head is still a mystery (pp. 38–39). Whalers had no problems finding a use for the oil. These spermaceti oil candles burn with a bright, clear flame. Engravings of Yankee whalers often show them bathed in the light of a thousand such lamps and candles.

SPERMACETI CANDLES
from
NANTUCKET ISLAND, MASS.

### UMBRELLA

Old umbrellas had ribs made of springy baleen. Nowadays these have been replaced with steel or plastic.

*Baleen ribs*

### GET YOUR WHALE MEAT!

With the advent of plastics and petroleum, the market for whale products almost disappeared. Now the main product is whale meat for eating. This Norwegian fishing boat has caught a whale to supplement its income. Some of the meat is sold locally on the wharf, but most is exported to Japan.

ONE PAIR    DAWBARN'S    BLA-
**Genuine WHITE WHALE Boot Laces**
HAND-CUT    WALONGA BRAND    NO TAGS
MADE IN ENGLAND    MARKET HARBOROUGH, LEICESTERSHIRE
These Laces should not be pulled or jerked violently when first placed in the shoes

### BELUGA BOOTLACES

These bootlaces were made from the skin of belugas (white whales, p. 37). Whale oil was used to soften all kinds of leather.

Whale meat extract

Whale meal

Whale liver oil

Sperm oil

*Dyed baleen bristles ready to be made into brushes*

### RAW MATERIALS

Whale meat extract was used to manufacture margarine. Animal feed and pet food were made from whale meal. Whale liver oil was a source of vitamin A, and sperm oil was a machine lubricant.

*Handle made from whale's bone*

# Seal hunting

*Flint spearhead*

**MOVING TARGET**
The Inuit hunted seals from small sealskin boats called kayaks. The harpoon line was attached to a float, a seal bladder blown up like a balloon. If the harpooned seal put up a struggle, the hunter would throw the line and float overboard rather than risk capsizing the kayak.

Lᴵᴋᴇ ᴡʜᴀʟᴇs, seals have been hunted for centuries. The story of sealing is not as well known, but it is just as bloody. The Inuit (Eskimo) people of the Arctic have always hunted seals. They made use of every bit of the seal, eating its meat, making clothes and boats from its skin, and burning seal oil in lamps. They never killed a lot of seals. But in the last two centuries, reckless commercial hunting did great damage to many seal populations. In the southern oceans, millions of elephant and fur seals were killed.

Huge numbers of walruses died in the Arctic, and the northern elephant seal was brought within a whisker of extinction (p. 41). But unlike whales, many seal populations have recovered. Sealing continues today, but the market for seal products is small.

*Bone harpoon*

*Shaft carved from a whale penis bone*

Inuit stone sculpture of seal hunter, from northern Canada

*Head carved from seal bone*

*Wooden paw*

**ICE SCRATCHER**
Another way hunters caught seals was to build a small shelter on the ice right next to a breathing hole. The Inuit hunter would stand by the hole for hours on end, a harpoon raised and ready to strike. To stop his feet from freezing, he stood on a folded sealskin. The first sign of a seal would be the sound of its breathing. This scratcher from Alaska was rubbed on the ice to attract curious seals to the surface.

*Soapstone*

*Bone knife*

*Seal breathing hole*

*Hunter dragging dead seal*

**SEALING SCENE**
This seal hunting scene was etched onto a walrus tusk (pp. 42–43). The successful hunters are dragging dead seals with harpoon lines. Many Inuit myths are about seals. They believe that seals are always thirsty, so when one is killed, the hunter puts water to its lips.

*Open sea*   *Hunter in kayak*

*Harpoon thrower*

*Figure of hunter*

*Wooden handle*

**HARPOON**
Wood is scarce in the Arctic. This harpoon is made from driftwood, stone, and whale bones.

**MODEL HUNTER**
This model of a man in a kayak shows the various harpoons and other implements of a seal hunter. Inuit men first made models like this for their children to play with. Later they gave them to European whalers and sealers in exchange for guns or metal tools.

*Harpoon lashed to deck*

**WALRUS HUNT**
As soon as Europeans arrived in Canada, they started killing seals. Huge numbers of walruses were shot from boats for their oil, tusks, and leather.

**NASTY PICK**
Seals have thin skulls. Sealers in the Arctic used picks like this to kill their prey with a quick blow to the head.

**LAST MOMENTS**
The killing of harp seals in Canada for their fur became an international controversy. Many people think the hunt is cruel and wasteful. The seals are clubbed on the head, and pups are often killed in front of their mothers. Hunters take only the fur and leave the body.

**GRIZZLY TRADE**
These sealers are hacking tusks out of walruses' heads. Walruses were the first seals to be hunted commercially, because they gather in huge herds. When there were almost none left, the sealers turned to gray seals. These are much smaller, but they still contain a lot of valuable oil.

**WILD GRAFFITI**
Conservation and animal welfare groups campaigned to end the harp seal hunt. Film of the seal hunt was shown on TV all over the world. This worker is spraying a pup with dye. This will make its fur worthless to hunters, who may spare it.

Purse made from seal fur

**MONEY TALKS**
Pressure from conservationists led the European Community to ban harp and hooded seal products. Many Canadians are very bitter about this. They claim that the seals are not endangered and should be killed because they eat valuable fish.

Harp seal pup

# Myths and legends

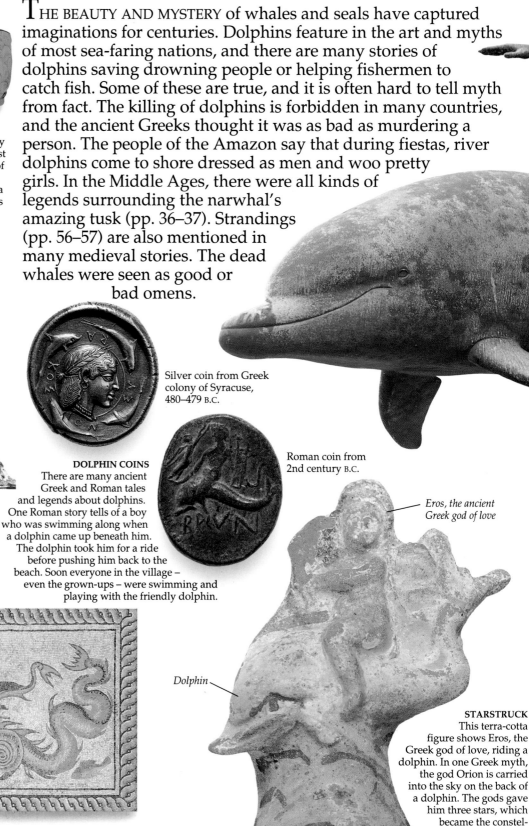

THE BEAUTY AND MYSTERY of whales and seals have captured imaginations for centuries. Dolphins feature in the art and myths of most sea-faring nations, and there are many stories of dolphins saving drowning people or helping fishermen to catch fish. Some of these are true, and it is often hard to tell myth from fact. The killing of dolphins is forbidden in many countries, and the ancient Greeks thought it was as bad as murdering a person. The people of the Amazon say that during fiestas, river dolphins come to shore dressed as men and woo pretty girls. In the Middle Ages, there were all kinds of legends surrounding the narwhal's amazing tusk (pp. 36–37). Strandings (pp. 56–57) are also mentioned in many medieval stories. The dead whales were seen as good or bad omens.

**GOLD KILLER**
This gold killer whale box was carved by Bill Reid. He is part Haida, from the west coast of Canada. The Haida tell stories of the evil ocean people, who used killer whales as canoes. One day they turned a Haida chief into a killer whale. Now this whale protects the Haida from attacks.

**FLIPPER, KING OF THE SEA**
The first whale to become a TV star was Flipper, a bottle-nosed dolphin. When people were in trouble and needed rescuing, Flipper was always there to save the day. Flipper's special friend was a young boy.

Silver coin from Greek colony of Syracuse, 480–479 B.C.

**DOLPHIN COINS**
There are many ancient Greek and Roman tales and legends about dolphins. One Roman story tells of a boy who was swimming along when a dolphin came up beneath him. The dolphin took him for a ride before pushing him back to the beach. Soon everyone in the village – even the grown-ups – were swimming and playing with the friendly dolphin.

Roman coin from 2nd century B.C.

Eros, the ancient Greek god of love

Dolphin

**NEPTUNE'S FRIEND**
In this ancient Roman mosaic from a villa in North Africa, a dolphin is carrying Neptune's trident. Neptune was the god of the sea, the Roman version of the Greek god Poseidon. Here he is shown as part horse, part fish, and part man.

**STARSTRUCK**
This terra-cotta figure shows Eros, the Greek god of love, riding a dolphin. In one Greek myth, the god Orion is carried into the sky on the back of a dolphin. The gods gave him three stars, which became the constellation Orion's Belt.

## BOY AND DOLPHIN

Solitary dolphins around the world seem to seek out human company. They often develop special relationships with certain people and spend hours playing with them. Through history there are many stories of dolphins rescuing drowning people. Some of them are probably true.

Statue of boy and dolphin by English artist David Wynne ( born 1926)

## STOMACH FULL

In real life, Jonah could never have survived for three days in the belly of a whale (p. 12). There would be no air to breathe, and he would suffocate quickly. There is a story of a 19th-century whaler who was swallowed by a sperm whale and found alive when the whale was killed several hours later. Could this incredible story be true?

## SEAL STORIES

In many seal legends, the seal disguises itself as a person. In the Orkney Islands off the north coast of Scotland, they tell stories of "selchies." These seals come ashore and behave like people. One story tells of a hunter who married a beautiful girl he met on the beach. One day, she found her fur coat, which he had hidden after they met. She put it on, turned into a seal, and swam away. Tragically, her husband later killed her on a hunting trip.

## GREEK SEA LION

This fanciful sea lion has the head of a lion, the hooves of a horse, and the tail of a dolphin.

## OUT OF THE BIG BLUE

This is the poster for *The Big Blue*, a 1988 film by the French writer and director Luc Besson. It is the story of two divers, each trying to dive deeper than the other. One is cheery and sociable; the other gets along better with dolphins than people. With its superb underwater photography, *The Big Blue* made millions of people interested in dolphins.

Ancient Greek black figure jar with sea lion, 500–470 B.C.

# Strandings and whale watching

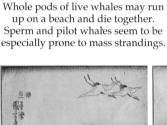

UNTIL RECENTLY, most people only saw big whales dead on the beach. This is called stranding. A stranded whale always attracts a crowd. Usually the whale has died at sea and has washed up on the shore. But every year, many live whales swim out of the water and strand themselves. Why they do this is still a mystery. Rescuers try to save the whales by covering them with wet towels. This keeps them cool and stops their sensitive skins from burning. When the tide comes in, the whales are helped to swim free. But often they head straight back to the beach and strand again. These days, many people head out to sea to watch live whales. This is a growing industry in many countries.

**STRANDED PILOT**
Whole pods of live whales may run up on a beach and die together. Sperm and pilot whales seem to be especially prone to mass strandings.

Huge baleen whale stranded on an English beach in 1924

**WHY DO THEY DO IT?**
People have all sorts of explanations for live stranding. Some say that families strand together because one member of the group is ill. The whales may be lost or disoriented. But because we do not really know how they navigate, this is hard to prove. Strandings of dead whales may be caused by pollution (pp. 58–59), which weakens resistance to disease. Recent "die-offs" of dolphins in the Mediterranean and off the east coast of North America support this theory.

*The Stranded Whale*, a woodblock print by the Japanese artist Kuniyoshi, about 1851

**SAVED, LIVE ON TELEVISION**
When winter approaches and the water begins to freeze, whales can become trapped by the advancing ice (pp. 36–37). In 1988, an international rescue was organized to save three gray whales trapped in the Arctic. Inuit workers kept the breathing hole open with chainsaws, while the whole world watched on television. Finally, Russian icebreaker ships cleared a safe path to the sea.

### ROYAL FISHES
Since the 14th century, all whales stranded in Britain have officially belonged to the king or queen and are called "Fishes Royal." This pleased Elizabeth I, who was fond of whale meat. In recent years, all strandings where reported to the coast guard. Because of these laws, Britain has kept very good stranding records.

### CROWD PULLER
On land, a dead whale's blubber insulates its body, so it warms up and decomposes fast. This is very smelly. The carcass becomes bloated with gases which make the whale more round. This huge sperm whale stranded on a Dutch beach in 1601. The local people thought it was an evil omen.

### PERFORMING ANIMAL
Many people feel that marine parks are cruel circuses where the animals are trained to perform unnatural tricks. Their pools are tiny compared to the open ocean. It is very difficult to keep captive whales in good health, and many live short lives. For these reasons, people in some countries have campaigned against marine parks. In Australia, the government has suggested that they be phased out.

# Watching whales

Around the world, there are many places to go whale watching. In some countries this is becoming a bigger industry than whaling ever was. In Japan and Norway, trips are led by ex-whalers. The gray whales in California are so friendly you can touch them from your canoe. In South Africa, it is forbidden to approach whales in boats, so people watch them from the shore. One town has a "whale crier" whose job is to let people know which bay the whales are in.

### CLOSE TO A KILLER
At marine parks, people can come and see dolphins or killer whales. They provide the only chance for many people to see a whale. Our attitude to whales has changed partly because so many people have been able to enjoy them close up.

### WHOA!
Imagine watching a humpback leap right beside your boat. In some places whale watching is big business. Many boats provide spaces for scientists who can study the whales at the same time.

# Fishing and pollution

Now that most countries have stopped hunting them, the biggest threats whales and seals face are fishing and pollution. Every year, hundreds of thousands of whales and seals are drowned when they become tangled in fishing nets. The fishermen often view the mammals as pests. In countries like Norway and Canada, overfishing by people has reduced fish stocks. But the fishermen blame seals and whales for the problem and campaign for hunts to keep their numbers down (p. 53). Some people are concerned that the oceans are being used as a dump for the poisonous chemicals produced by industry. Once toxic chemicals have been released into the sea, it is impossible to recover them. They are invisible but deadly. Whales and seals are particularly at risk because pollutants collect in their fat.

**NO ACCIDENT**
Seals and whales are usually tangled in nets by accident. But this Russian hunter has used a net to catch a rare Baikal seal (p. 63). He will sell the meat for food and the fur to make coats and hats.

**DOLPHIN TRAP**
Trawlers catch fish by dragging nets like this one through the water. When two boats trawl together, the nets are so big that a whole school of dolphins could swim in and get caught.

**INTO THE AIR AND SEA**
Most methods of making paper produce highly poisonous chemicals. This is one of the paper mills that dump waste into the world's largest freshwater lake, Lake Baikal in Russia. It is home to the endangered Baikal seal.

**WHALE-SIZED MESS**
Everyone is horrified when an oil tanker is wrecked and pours its oil into the sea. Clean-up teams can usually recover only a small part of the oil. It is much more important to prevent such disasters from happening in the first place.

**SWIMMING IN OIL**
When a sea otter (p. 7) gets covered in oil, its fur becomes matted. The animal has trouble keeping warm and may die of cold. In a desperate attempt to lick itself clean, the otter will also swallow poisonous oil. Hundreds of rare sea otters were hurt or killed in the *Exxon Valdez* oil spill in Alaska in 1989. Oil damages habitats and poisons food supplies. Oil poured into the Persian Gulf during the Gulf War of 1991 harmed the sea grass beds where dugongs feed. No one knows what the long-term effects of such huge spills will be.

**INVISIBLE POISONS**
Many poisonous chemicals are dumped into the sea. Some are pesticides such as DDT. These are passed up the food chain and concentrated in the bodies of predators like seals and whales. We now know that female whales pass these pollutants directly to their young through their milk.

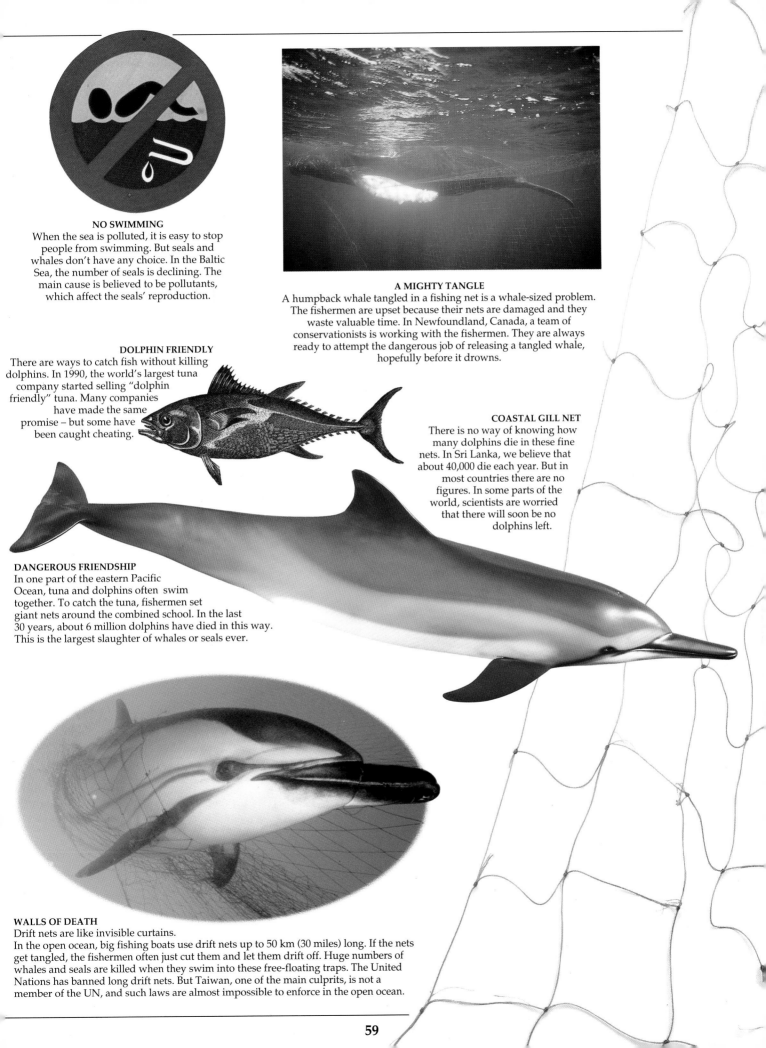

## NO SWIMMING
When the sea is polluted, it is easy to stop people from swimming. But seals and whales don't have any choice. In the Baltic Sea, the number of seals is declining. The main cause is believed to be pollutants, which affect the seals' reproduction.

## A MIGHTY TANGLE
A humpback whale tangled in a fishing net is a whale-sized problem. The fishermen are upset because their nets are damaged and they waste valuable time. In Newfoundland, Canada, a team of conservationists is working with the fishermen. They are always ready to attempt the dangerous job of releasing a tangled whale, hopefully before it drowns.

## DOLPHIN FRIENDLY
There are ways to catch fish without killing dolphins. In 1990, the world's largest tuna company started selling "dolphin friendly" tuna. Many companies have made the same promise – but some have been caught cheating.

## COASTAL GILL NET
There is no way of knowing how many dolphins die in these fine nets. In Sri Lanka, we believe that about 40,000 die each year. But in most countries there are no figures. In some parts of the world, scientists are worried that there will soon be no dolphins left.

## DANGEROUS FRIENDSHIP
In one part of the eastern Pacific Ocean, tuna and dolphins often swim together. To catch the tuna, fishermen set giant nets around the combined school. In the last 30 years, about 6 million dolphins have died in this way. This is the largest slaughter of whales or seals ever.

## WALLS OF DEATH
Drift nets are like invisible curtains.
In the open ocean, big fishing boats use drift nets up to 50 km (30 miles) long. If the nets get tangled, the fishermen often just cut them and let them drift off. Huge numbers of whales and seals are killed when they swim into these free-floating traps. The United Nations has banned long drift nets. But Taiwan, one of the main culprits, is not a member of the UN, and such laws are almost impossible to enforce in the open ocean.

# Studying sea mammals

WE STILL KNOW VERY LITTLE about the lives of seals and whales. The first information on anatomy came from cutting up dead animals, and the contents of the stomach or ovaries gave clues on diet or reproduction. More recently, many new techniques that do not harm animals have been developed. Some involve photography; others require small tissue samples. Whales live in a world of sound (pp. 26–27), and an underwater microphone can be used to find, follow, and even count them. One of the hardest questions to answer is: "How many whales are there?" Scientists and mathematicians have been working on this problem for three decades. But we still have only rough estimates for the size of most populations.

French engraving from 19th century showing scientists studying a model whale

**JACQUES COUSTEAU**
This French adventurer has made many popular films and books about life under the sea.

la baleine
sel de mer fin
iodé fluoré

DESIGN LONSDALE

**DNA FINGERPRINTING**
Scientists can now use a small piece of skin or muscle to identify an individual animal. They do this by examining the animal's DNA, its unique genetic material. The result, a "DNA fingerprint," looks something like a bar code. Scientists can then use the bands to identify close relatives, for example an animal's parents or sisters.

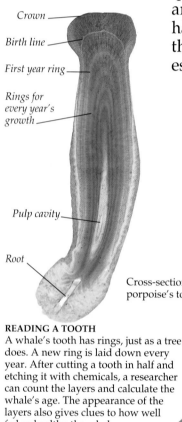

*Crown*

*Birth line*

*First year ring*

*Rings for every year's growth*

*Pulp cavity*

*Root*

Cross-section of harbor porpoise's tooth

**WHALES ALIVE**
One of the best way to study whales in their element is from small sailboats (motorboats can make a lot of noise). Researchers take photos to identify individuals. Microphones left under the water follow the whales' vocalizations. The whales' social life can be pieced together from all this information.

**READING A TOOTH**
A whale's tooth has rings, just as a tree does. A new ring is laid down every year. After cutting a tooth in half and etching it with chemicals, a researcher can count the layers and calculate the whale's age. The appearance of the layers also gives clues to how well fed or healthy the whale was from one year to the next.

*Nicks caused by parasites, fights, or collisions with boats*

*Scratches from other dolphin's teeth*

**HERE'S MY I.D.**
Every humpback whale has a unique black-and-white pattern on the underside of its tail. Thousands of humpbacks have been photographed and their patterns recorded and cataloged. Every time a whale is sighted, its pattern is checked against the catalog to see if it has been spotted before. This allows scientists to count populations, follow whales as they migrate, and learn whom they spend their time with.

**SCRATCHED AND SCARRED**
Whales collect scratches and scars as they swim through life. These telltale marks can be used to identify individual animals. This is easier with old whales, like this 25-year-old bottle-nosed dolphin, which have more scars. The problem is that marks may change, which makes identification uncertain!

### EARLY DISSECTION

Much of our early information on whales comes from the whaling industry. Early whalers and scientists recorded very detailed information on the gigantic corpses. Now most of the questions that remain can only be answered by studying live animals.

*Radio antenna*

*Remnants of molted fur*

Used satellite tag with molted fur

### ON THE PULSE

This acoustic transmitter broadcasts the heartbeat. The beat changes drastically when the animal goes for a deep dive.

*Sensor which shows how deep seal is diving and how fast it is swimming*

### SATELLITE TAG

When the animal surfaces, the data stored in this transmitter is beamed to a satellite and on to the lab.

*VHF tag which sends out a radio signal*

Acoustic tag

# Tags for tracking

How do you follow a seal or a whale without getting wet? One way is to attach a tag to its body. This can then send back information on where the animal goes, how fast it swims, and how deep it dives. The most sophisticated tags send their signals to satellites. These tags are expensive, but their signals can be tracked anywhere in the world.

### SEEING UNDER THE SEA

This computer-generated map shows the movements of a tagged elephant seal. One seal swam an incredible 1,640 miles (2,650 km) in 70 days. This seal is looking for food along the edge of the continental shelf. Every vertical white line is a dive.

*Tip of Antarctic continent*

*Sea level*

*Path of seal*

*Sea bottom over continental shelf*

*Edge of continental shelf*

### FOLLOWING HIS NOSE

Attaching tags to seals or whales is not an easy job. This big male elephant seal (pp. 40–41) has a tag glued to his head. When he molts in the spring, the tag will fall off with his old fur. Other tags are shot into the skin of whales. But some people think this is cruel.

*Deep ocean bottom*

# Save the whale!

THE FUTURE OF WHALES and seals depends on people from all over the world cooperating. The seas are a common resource. How should they be used? Will it ever be possible to catch whales humanely and without hunting them to extinction? Can we develop whale tourism instead? Is it cruel to keep dolphins in captivity (p. 57)? How can we control pollution and the use of fishing nets (pp. 58–59)? It is even difficult to reach agreement about which species are endangered. Many countries have different views on all these questions – usually for their own reasons. Because whales migrate, they do not just belong to the countries that want to hunt them. The only way forward is by international cooperation, rational discussion, and responsible research. People are becoming more aware of the problems, but this is only the first step. Good intentions must be followed by real action and commitment. Only then can we safeguard the future of these magnificent animals.

**STAMP DUTY**
Developing countries are becoming aware of conservation problems. These stamps from Sri Lanka show some of the country's marine mammals.

Whale drawing
by Liam Bleach, age 5

Blue whale drawn
by Domoniqua Douglas,
age 5

**STARTING EARLY**
The best way to change attitudes toward whales and seals is to get children interested at an early age. These days most children know a lot about environmental issues. Often they have to teach their parents!

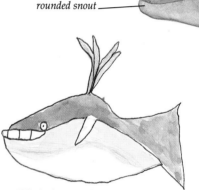

Distinctive short,
rounded snout

Whale drawing by
Giuseppe Paese, age 6

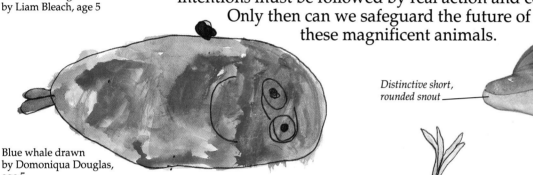

**ABORIGINAL WHALING**
With a leap from his wooden boat, a man drives a long bamboo pole into a whale. Only two villages in Indonesia still hunt whales in this way. Elsewhere in the world, a few whales are still caught in traditional ways in Tonga, Alaska, and Bequia in the Caribbean. Hundreds of narwhals and belugas are killed every year in Greenland (pp. 36–37).

**MASS SLAUGHTER**
In the Færoe Islands in the North Atlantic between Scotland and Iceland, whole pods of pilot whales are still hunted. The whales are driven ashore and killed. There has been an international outcry against the hunt, and the hunters have been portrayed as cruel. But because the complaints come from outside the islands, the Færoese have become more determined than ever to continue the yearly hunt.

# Endangered species

A few species of whale and seal are close to disappearing forever. There are few blue whales left in the southern oceans (pp. 20–21). The areas they roam are so vast that they may not be able to find a mate! Gray whales were almost extinct by 1946. Now the California population has gone up to about 20,000.

**RIGHT WHALES**
The right whales are all threatened by extinction. The rarest of all, the bowhead, is still hunted in small numbers in Alaska (p. 49). Slow-moving northern right whales are often killed when they are hit by boats. One bright spot is South Africa, where southern right whales are becoming more common.

**AMAZON RIVER DOLPHIN**
This Amazon River dolphin was killed by a fisherman. Several species of river dolphin are on the verge of extinction (p. 33). A dam has divided the Indus River species into two populations. Only a miracle will save the Chinese river dolphin. There are less than 200 left in the entire Changjiang (Yangtze River) system.

**LAKE BAIKAL SEAL**
We now know what needs to be done to save some species, such as this Baikal seal. It is threatened by pollution and will only survive if paper mills stop pouring poisons into Lake Baikal (p. 58). For many other species of seal, there are no easy answers. The numbers of certain species, such as the Steller's sea lion (pp. 23, 30–31) and the southern elephant seal (pp. 40–41), are going down. No one is sure why this is happening, or what to do to save them.

**SET FREE**
The welfare of captive animals is now an issue in some countries (p. 57). Many marine parks were built decades ago and no longer meet new standards. These dolphins, Silver and Missie, used to live in an underground marine park in Brighton, England. When the old building was sold, the new owners decided to return the animals to the wild.

*Pale gray color, darker on back and turning to white on belly*

**BACK TO THE OPEN OCEAN**
After months of planning, the two dolphins were carried in slings into an airplane and flown to an island in the Caribbean. They spent several months in a fenced-off lagoon learning how to catch live fish. Then they were set free.

*The bottlenose dolphin is the largest dolphin, growing up to 13 ft (4 m) long and weighing as much as 1,450 lb (650 kg)*

# Index

# Acknowledgments

**Vassili Papastavrou** would like to dedicate this book to Catherine and thank Mel Brooks, Nigel & Jennifer Bonner, Tom Arnbom, Bill Amos, Denise Herzing, Graham Leach, Gill Hartley, Simon Hay and Nick Davies.

**Dorling Kindersley would like to thank** Jon Kershaw & the staff of Marineland, Antibes, France; Ron Kastelein & the staff of Harderwijk Marine Mammal Park, Holland; Adrian Friday & Ray Symonds at University Museum of Zoology, Cambridge, for skeletons (pp. 12, 13, 23, 25, 36, 40, 43); Bob Headland at Scott Polar Institute, Cambridge, for the harpoon gun (pp. 48–49); John Ward at the British Antarctic Survey for the krill (p. 25); Arthur Credland at Town Docks Museum, Hull for the whaling artefacts (pp. 46–53); John Shearer for the nets (pp. 56–57); the Sea Mammal Research Unit, Cambridge, esp. Christine Lockyer for the tooth (p. 60) & Kevin Nicholas & Bernie McConnell for the tags (p. 61); Sarah Richardson and the pupils of Townsend Primary School, London (p. 62); Jocelyn Steedman in Vancouver; Helena Spiteri for editorial help; Sharon Spencer, Manisha Patel and Jabu Mahlangu for design help.

**Additional photography:** Harry Taylor, Natural History Museum, London; Ivor Curzlake, British Museum, London (pp. 2–3, 33 & 54–55); Dave King (pp. 6, 10tl, 32–33 & 62–63) and Jerry Young (p. 7).

**Index**: Céline Carez

### Picture credits

t = top, b = bottom, c = center, l = left, r = right

American Museum of Natural History, New York 20-21; Ancient Art & Architecture Collection 6tl, 36tl, 46tl; Aquarius Library / MGM 54cl; Ardea London Limited / F. Gohier 18tl, 56b; Tom Arnbom 41tl, 41tr; Auscape International / D. Parer & E. Parer-Cook 34cr, 34br; Baleine Blanche French School Afloat /G. Hartley 60c; Barnaby's Picture Library / W. Lüthy 48tl / N.D. Price 51cla; BFI / © Gaumont 1988 55bl; Bibliothèque Nationale, Paris / Gallimard Jeunesse 12bc; Nigel Bonner 48bl; Bridgeman Art Library / Giraudon 32tl / Private Collection 55tr, 57tl; Staatlich Antikens-ammlung, Munich 2tr; British Museum, London 42tr; Bruce Coleman Limited; Corbis Stock Market: Dr I. Everson 41cl / J. Foott 7bl, 35tr, 46br, 53b / F. Lanting 35cr / N. Lightfoot 53ca / D. & M. Plage 58b / Dr E. Potts 37cr / H. Reinhard: 43tl; R. Ellis 62bl; E.T. Archive 53tc; Mary Evans Picture Library 32tr, 34tl, 36bl, 37tl, 42cl, 48br, 50tl, 55bl, 63tr. Werner Forman Archive / Field Museum of Natural History, USA 52cla; Greenpeace / Culley 49br / Gleizes 53cr / Martenson 59tl / Rowlands 59bl; © Hergé 9cr; Michael Holford 32bl, 56cl; I.F.A.W. 31cr; Jacana / F. Gohier 20cl, 21cr; Kendall Whaling Museum, Sharon, Mass. / USA 50cl, 51clb; Frank Lane Picture Agency / T. Stephenson 63tl; Peter Lugårch 40cl; Mail Newspapers / Solo Syndication 63bl; Marineland / J. Foudraz 29tr, 29c; Minden Pictures / © F. Nicklin 39tr; Musée d'Histoire Naturelle, Paris / Gallimard Jeunesse 12bc; Natural History Museum, London 8tl, 9br, 10ca, 10cb, 20b, 36-37, 56cr; NHPA / B. & C. Alexander 59tc / D. Currey 62tr / P. Johnson 29crb; / T. Nakuniara 30cl; O.S.F / D. Allan 18cl, 25b, 37tr, 37cra, 49tl, 58tl, 58tr, 63cr / D. Fleetham 26bl / L.E. Lauber 28cl / T. Martin 49tr; Pacific Whale Foundation / © 1990 D. Moses 57br; V. Papastavrou 12tl, 38br; Planet Earth Pictures / J. King 38bl / Menuhin 18tr / F. Schulke 60tr / M. Snyderman 20cr, 33clb / J. D. Watt 6cl; Rex Features Limited / E. Thorburn 27tr / Roger-Viollet 21tr; Ann Ronan at Image Select 47tl, 48tr; Courtesy of the Royal British Columbia Museum, Victoria, B.C., Canada / B. Reid 54tr; Science Photo Library / European Space Agency 39tl; Sea Life Cruises / R. Fairbairns 17c; Sea Mammal Research Unit, Cambridge / Dr C. Lockyer 61bl; C. Hunter 61crb / Dr T Martin 56tl, 60cr, 62br; Service Historique de la Marine, Vincennes / Gallimard Jeunesse 6bl; Frank Spooner Pictures / Gamma 58cl; S. Steedman 57cl; Texas A & M University at Galveston / Dr B. Würsig 32br; Wild Dolphin Project Inc. / D. Herzing 29tl, 31tl.